G000270623

Praise for *Van Diemen's Land*

'The most significant colonial history since *The Fatal Shore*.
In re-imagining Australia's past, it invents a new future.'
Richard Flanagan

'A revisionist version of Tasmania's past, *Van Diemen's Land* by
James Boyce moves away from the usual history of genocide
to examine the phenomenon of a white underclass taking on
Aboriginal ways of living – an unusual version of a familiar tale.'
The Observer, Best Books of the Year, 2008

'Tasmania is only a short flight from where I live, but
I have never been there. Now I will go, because its
grasslands, mountains, bays and islands have become
real to me, each territory with its own history and
bearing the subtle scars of its particular past.'
Inga Clendinnen, *London Review of Books*

'A fresh and sparkling account'
Henry Reynolds, *The Age*

'Boyce's *Van Diemen's Land* is a triumph'
The Sydney Morning Herald

'[A] remarkable work'
The Canberra Times

'[P]assionate and comprehensive'
Australian Book Review

Praise for *Born Bad*

'Ambitious, thought-provoking … an easy read
on an ignored but central and timely topic.'
The Tablet

'This is an exceptional, highly recommended work,
innovative and creative in surprising ways.'
Publishers Weekly, starred review, April 2015

'James Boyce has … written a brilliant and exhilarating
work of popular scholarship. I pencil vertical lines in
the margins of the books I read whenever a sentence or
paragraph seems especially striking. My copy of *Born
Bad* carries such scribbles on every other page.'
Michael Dirda, *Washington Post*

'Boyce covers a lot of ground and explores a number
of authors in this wide-ranging treatment, and the
result is impressive. Readable and comprehensive …
Boyce successfully illustrates the ability of original sin to
dominate Western culture for nearly two millennia.'
Kirkus, April 2015

'An imaginative and utterly unpredictable book. Alleluia'
The Australian

'James Boyce is the best kind of historian of ideas. He
does not reduce the complexity of his ideas to a few
easy lessons … [Here] is an unblinking regard for the
efforts the human race has made to understand itself.'
The Age

ALSO BY JAMES BOYCE

Van Diemen's Land (Black Inc, 2008). Winner of the
Colin Roderick Award and Tasmania Book Prize. A tenth
anniversary edition, with an introduction by Richard Flanagan,
was released in October 2018.

1835: The Founding of Melbourne and the Conquest of Australia
(Black Inc, 2011). Winner of the Tasmania Book Prize and
The Age Book of the Year, 2012

Born Bad: Original Sin and the Making of the Western World
(Black Inc, 2014; US edition, Counterpoint Press, 2015;
UK edition, SPCK, 2016).

Losing Streak: How Tasmania was Gamed by the Gambling Industry
(Black Inc, 2017). Winner of the People's Choice Award,
Tasmania Book Prize, 2017.

IMPERIAL MUD

The Fight for the Fens

JAMES BOYCE

This project has been assisted by the Australian Government through the Australia Council, its arts funding and advisory body.

ICON

Published in the UK in 2020 by
Icon Books Ltd, Omnibus Business Centre,
39–41 North Road, London N7 9DP
email: info@iconbooks.com
www.iconbooks.com

Sold in the UK, Europe and Asia
by Faber & Faber Ltd, Bloomsbury House,
74–77 Great Russell Street,
London WC1B 3DA or their agents

Distributed in the UK, Europe and Asia
by Grantham Book Services,
Trent Road, Grantham NG31 7XQ

Distributed in Australia and New Zealand
by Allen & Unwin Pty Ltd, PO Box 8500,
83 Alexander Street, Crows Nest, NSW 2065

Distributed in the USA by Publishers Group West,
1700 Fourth Street, Berkeley, CA 94710

Distributed in Canada by Publishers Group Canada,
76 Stafford Street, Unit 300, Toronto, Ontario M6J 2S1

Distributed in South Africa by
Jonathan Ball, Office B4, The District,
41 Sir Lowry Road, Woodstock 7925

Distributed in India by Penguin Books India,
7th Floor, Infinity Tower – C, DLF Cyber City,
Gurgaon 122002, Haryana

ISBN: 978-178578-650-1

Text copyright © 2020 James Boyce

Typeset in Bembo by Marie Doherty

Printed and bound in Great Britain
by Clays Ltd, Elcograf S.p.A.

CONTENTS

ABOUT THE AUTHOR

James Boyce is a multi-award-winning Australian historian. His first book, *Van Diemen's Land*, was described by Richard Flanagan as 'the most significant colonial history since *The Fatal Shore*'. *1835: The Founding of Melbourne and the Conquest of Australia* was *The Age*'s Book of the Year, while *Born Bad: Original Sin and the Making of the Western World* was hailed by *The Washington Post* as 'an exhilarating work of popular scholarship'.

To William:
Whose ancestors made home in the Fens.

LIST OF ILLUSTRATIONS

MAPS

THE CAMBRIDGESHIRE & NORFOLK FENS

THE LINCOLNSHIRE FENS

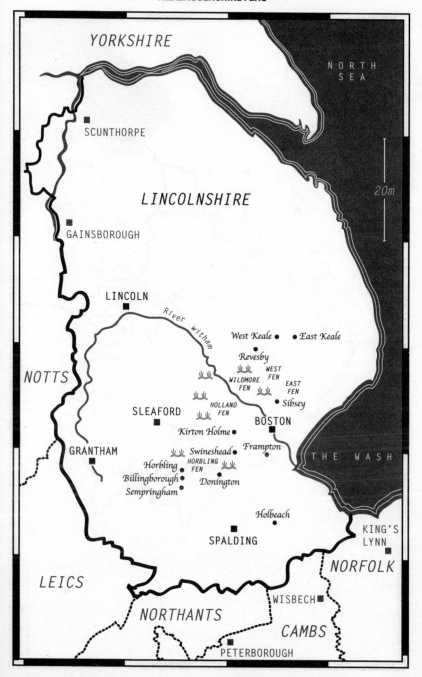

THE ISLE OF AXHOLME

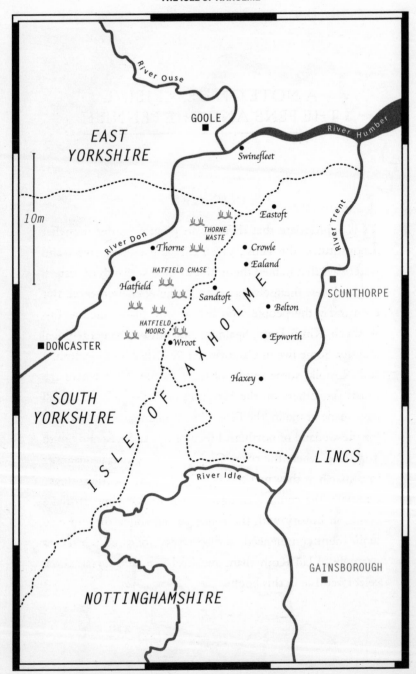

A NOTE ON DESCRIBING
THE FENS AND THE FENNISH

It is appropriate that there is no precise border for what constitutes 'the Fens', given that the creeks, rivers and waterways that framed the near-vanished wetlands of eastern England were themselves an ever-changing phenomenon. But even today the people who live around places such as Ely, Wisbech, King's Lynn, Spalding and Boston share a regional identity. Some live in Cambridgeshire, others in Lincolnshire and Norfolk; some reside adjacent to the Wash where the soil is silt, others on the famously rich peat inland; but all have made home in 'the Fens'. The nomenclature is less clear for the wetland of northern Lincolnshire and East and South Yorkshire, where the rivers Ouse and Trent used to meander into marsh as they met the Humber. These 'northern fens', especially the country around the Isle of Axholme, shared a common history with the southern fens once the move to drain them commenced, and so I have followed the recent example of Ian Rotherham and Eric Ash, and included the celebrated Isle in this book.

While people from the Fens shared a regional identity, there is wide divergence of practice in how to describe them. A twelfth-century chronicler of Ely mentions the 'Gyrwe', who were 'all the southern Angles that inhabit the great marsh'.[1] William Camden in *Britannia* (1586) said those that 'inhabit the fennish country ... were even in the Saxon times called Girvij, that is ... Fen-men or Fen-dwellers'. Samuel Pepys and Thomas Macaulay opted for 'breedlings'; Thomas Fuller and W.H. Wheeler for 'slodgers'. The term 'fen tiger' (from the Welsh word 'tioga' for peasant) recurs but is most often used only for resistance fighters. 'Fenmen' was widely employed in the nineteenth and twentieth centuries but presumably in response to its now obvious limitations, Eric Ash has opted for the rarely used 'fenlanders'. This is preferable to the cumbersome 'people from the Fens', but while it describes the geographical identity, it doesn't describe the distinctive way of life that emerged in the wetlands. Impertinently, I have therefore created the term 'Fennish'. I do so provisionally, respecting that the people of the Fens, like us all, have always enjoyed a variety of identities, including those based on nation, county, manor, parish and village. While it was accepted that they were different from the surrounding uplanders, like most pre-industrial peoples, the Fennish primarily identified with their local community. As with indigenous people in colonised countries, a sense of unity was strengthened once the process of dispossession began. Resisting imperialism helped create a shared identity for diverse groups of Native Americans and Aboriginal Australians as it did for the people of the Fens.

Whatever name is preferred, while those who lived in the Fens from the time of the wetland's formation to the time of its destruction remain without a name, the continuity of their culture will be obscured. It is a nostalgic myth of modernity that the culture of 'real' indigenous people was fixed in pre-historic time. All cultures undergo times of upheaval as well as long periods of evolution. What characterises an indigenous culture is neither its uniformity nor immutability, but that it remains rooted in country as it experiences continuity *and* change.

FOREWORD

Until a few hundred years ago, the rivers that flowed from central England to the North Sea metamorphosed into a wetland wilderness as they approached the Wash. Encouraged by low gradient and high sediment, they broke their banks to meander into countless and ever-changing channels, forming vast reed-covered fens, shallow bird-friendly lakes and nutrient-rich summer meadows more akin to the Amazonian delta than the ordered agricultural landscape that the Fens have now become.

The drainage of about a million wild acres of marshland from the early seventeenth to the mid-nineteenth century largely destroyed this extraordinary ecosystem and the ancient culture of its custodians. It is now difficult to imagine what has been lost. The Fennish relationship with their muddy home is as foreign to the modern mind as the traditional connection to country of the Aboriginal people of Australia.

This book does not attempt to take an imaginative leap into a vanquished world but to convey a little of what the land meant to the people of the Fens by documenting their heroic defence of it. Even today, most history books present

Fenland history as one of technology overcoming the environment.[1] This surprisingly resilient narrative is one of progress from an era of flooding, hardship, malaria, and poverty to the enlightened age of drainage, flood control and economic and social development. Those who resisted the wetland destruction are reduced in such histories to old-fashioned country folk hopelessly fighting the irresistible forces of history. What is taken for granted (even by those who lament what has been lost) is that market forces and technological progress *inevitably* win out in the end.

In recent decades, across the former British empire, scholars have been revisiting the history of contact and conflict between colonisers and indigenous peoples. The conquest of settler countries is now recognised to have involved accommodation, adaptation *and* multifarious forms of resistance. Local people are no longer presented as passive victims but human beings who, even during awful suffering, never surrender agency. Similarly, the invaders are never *only* servants of the imperial project. What has been highlighted is that although actions can never be understood without reference to cultural norms and power realities, nothing that happened in the past was pre-determined. I hope to show that this truth is equally applicable to the history of the conquest and colonisation of the Fens.

The history of Fennish resistance is as old as the wetland itself. Marshlands are such difficult places to conquer that the bloody arrival of Romans, Anglo-Saxons, Danes and Normans didn't supplant those who *already* lived in the Fens.

Although influenced by new technologies and trade (and not untouched by war or conquerors' decrees) the Fennish were able to hold on to their land and culture as newcomers opted for nominal rule from the higher ground or assimilated with the environmentally-attuned locals. The changes produced by a new monarch or lord were generally not as significant as the continual adaptation required from climate change, sea level rise, or changes in bird and fish migrations. What evolved in the Fens was a distinctive indigenous way of life and outlook on the world that endured regardless of who formally ruled the marsh.

It was not until an altogether new type of invader arrived from around 1600, men who sought a total transformation of the wetland, that Fennish cultural and community life was seriously threatened. Drainage now meant 'enclosure' (the exclusive possession of land by those having title to it) and the extinguishment of common rights. But it took over 200 years to enclose the Fens because the local people fought back, and in some regions were able to successfully protect the common marshland for generations. This heroic defence of England's last lowland wilderness should not only be defined by its ultimate defeat. As will be seen, the fight for the Fens was much more than a forlorn footnote to a triumphant imperial tale.

CHAPTER 1

The Formation of the Fens and the Fennish

Across the planet, most famously in the Euphrates, Nile, Indus and Yangtze river deltas, human beings chose to settle down in the marsh. The twin ecosystems of coastal estuary and freshwater swamp provided a continual bounty of edible plants, fish, birds, shellfish and mammals for those who understood seasonal migrations.[1] Moreover, marsh-dwellers had access to sediment-rich grazing and cropping grounds during the drier months to complement the wild food supply.[2] Because waterways were the highways of the world, wetlands were also global centres of trade and innovation.

Given the advantages of marshland for sedentary human living, it is not surprising that when a particularly rich one emerged in the eastern lowland regions of the relatively new island of Britain about 4,000 years ago, it was soon well populated.

Much of eastern Britain became part of the North Sea as the climate warmed and sea levels rose. But other parts of the former forest, now decaying into peat, became a half-way country protruding barely above sea level, where incoming tidal salt water and outgoing fresh water met to form one of the most diverse environments in Europe. This stunning land-scape boasted the largest lowland lakes (or 'meres') in England, vast areas of wet meadow (grassland flooded and fertilised in the winter months), and fertile dry islands where humans could base themselves year-round.

The Fens were full of fish, eels and waterbirds, with the wild foods multiplying at the same time that farming was also being successfully refined. Both forms of food collection became integral to Fennish life, further evidence that, as James C. Scott has explored, there is no 'fateful line that separates hunting and foraging from agriculture', nor any empirical basis to the assumed superiority of farming for economic and cultural development.[3] A predictable and easily count-able grain harvest was more efficient for collecting taxes and asserting centralised authority, but this should not be equated with human progress. The 1,300-year-old Saxon chronicle *Beowulf* depicts the swamp as the 'vile abode' of the evil demon named Grendel, but this is indicative of how hard it was to subdue those living in the 'fell and the fen', not a reflection on wetland fecundity.[4]

The richness of the ancient fen is illustrated by the fact that the remnants of the oldest construction in the UK can still be seen in the mud. Not far from Peterborough are the well-preserved remains of a 3,000-year-old section of an elevated mile-long timber road that provided access to a platform the size of Wembley stadium. The Flag Fen causeway was in regular use for over a thousand years. Two miles away at Must Farm near Whittlesey, nine log boats have recently been found. The archaeologist who led the excavation, Francis Pryor, has observed that '[these] boats represent compelling evidence of a mass colonisation of the recently formed wetlands and reveal just how [quickly] people learned to thrive in a submerged terrain'.[5]

Flag Fen was also a sacred site. An enormous variety of metalwork, from intricate swords and valuable jewellery to mundane domestic products, were ritually deposited there. Pryor has imagined that 'some of the items must have been dropped into the waters with cheering crowds and much rejoicing; others might have marked the end of a long and distinguished life; still others were doubtless private acts of longing, regret or recrimination. All of human life is there, had we the power to see it.' Perhaps what is most remarkable is that in the succeeding Iron Age (which refers to the period from about 700 BC to the coming of the Romans in AD 43), when the waters rose again and many areas, including Flag Fen, were inundated, 'belief in the worth of throwing weapons into the water persisted'. Indeed, this practice would last another thousand years.[6] There must have been scores of Excaliburs, royal and humble, sustaining such a sacred landscape.

By the late Iron Age, there was almost no fen creature that humans did not know how to capture or cook. At a settlement site not far from Flag Fen, now known as Cat's Water, domestic refuse has been found that contains the bones of mallard, pelican, cormorant, heron, stork, mute swan, barnacle goose, teal, table duck, merganser, sea eagle, goshawk, buzzard, crane, coot and crow. Fish was also almost certainly widely eaten, although the archaeological record is inevitably limited.[7] By 300 BC, midden deposits show that the Fennish were enjoying the same diverse protein-rich diet that would sustain their health and culture for the next 2,000 years.

While there is a gap between the abandonment of Flag Fen and the founding of Cat's Water, this does not mean that there was an interruption in settlement. Similarly, the fact that many Iron Age hamlets were buried by mud in the fourth and fifth centuries AD is not evidence that the Fens were depopulated after this.[8] The Fennish necessarily adapted to a changing climate by abandoning some areas and colonising others. Their way of life was attuned to periodic flooding and permanent inundation, with buildings relatively easily replaced when old sites became too wet. The round house unearthed at Flag Fen had oak posts with walls woven from willow and hazel that were covered with a clay and straw mixture. By the Iron Age, houses were thatched with local reed rather than the Bronze Age turf, but the basic wattle and daub technique that utilised easily accessible local materials remained the foundation of vernacular architecture until modern times.

The continuity of Fennish culture has been obscured by the prominence given to conquest. There is no question that the Roman invasion of Britain in AD 43 had a dramatic impact in the Fens. It led to the final abandonment of ritual practice at Flag Fen, with the new Roman causeway going directly through the area. (What better statement of imperial mastery over the old rulers and their gods could there be than to have legionaries trampling over a sacred site?) According to the Roman historian Tacitus, the legions marched on this road to put down the celebrated British rebellion led by Boudicca in AD 60/61. Other accounts suggest that the causeway was constructed to help maintain order once the victors found, as others would after them, that controlling the Fens was a formidable task. Venerable Bede observed of the Fennish warriors that 'environed with fens and reed-plecks unpassable ... they feared not the invasion of the enemy'. Dio Cassius recorded how the Romans 'wandered into the pathless marshes and lost many of their soldiers'. He believed that the Britons were 'capable of enduring hunger and thirst, and hardships of every description' and 'when hiding in the marshes they abide there many days with their heads only out of the water'.[9]

Tribal elites lost power after Boudicca's defeat and most of the Fens came under at least nominal Roman rule. Boundaries between the Iceni, Corieltauvi and other tribes are no longer clear (and may never have been precise) but they seem to have been united in the uprising and would therefore have shared the consequences of defeat – villages burnt, stock taken, and captives abducted as slaves. No doubt many of the Fennish were used as forced labour to extend Roman roads, canals and fortresses, but their culture endured because a permanent

Roman presence could not extend far into the marshland itself. There must have been many isolated refuges where traditions were maintained, and community life rebuilt. Once the armed conquest was concluded, there were also opportunities from the new political and economic order as centralised Roman rule and improved transport facilitated the sale of fish and game. The invaders also brought useful goods and technologies, none more transformative than the metal spade.

The Romans colonised parts of the Fens with retired legionaries, and some historians have argued that the intermittent archaeological record proves that the region was depopulated when this occurred.[10] But as Garrick Fincham has observed, this interruption in the 'ceramic sequence' was most likely the result of communities losing access to imported goods once political turbulence broke down trade.[11] It is highly unlikely that people *ever* abandoned a region so rich in resources. More probable is that such a bountiful and isolated country became a sought-after refuge during and after the Roman invasion. Simple self-sufficiency based on perishable local materials may leave few artefacts, but the Fens provided a rare level of material and physical security in turbulent times.[12]

Perhaps the most profound change to the Fennish way of life brought about by the Roman invasion was the arrival of malaria, which the legionaries brought with them from other regions of the empire. However, even this unwelcome ailment, like floods and storms, had its upside. For centuries outsiders would fear spending time in the fen because of 'ague', while local people generally built up a level of resistance to it.

The Romans made a more positive contribution to Fennish life through flood control. The conquerors were experienced drainers and two of their major constructions, both known as 'Car Dyke', can still be seen along the edge of the western Fenland (in the Fens a 'dyke' is not the bank adjacent to the ditch, as it is in the Netherlands, but the ditch itself). One dyke ran north from the River Nene near Water Newton, past Bourne, to the Witham valley near Lincoln. It consisted of a low central channel about six feet deep and 40 feet wide with even wider banks on either side (which survive to about three feet above ground level today). The other dyke seems to have linked the River Cam with the Great Ouse and Old West River. The function of the Car Dykes is not clear. They may have been drains preventing fresh water from flooding the fens or they might have been canals for trade and military transport.[13]

Controlling water flows and mitigating flooding was not a Roman agenda alone. Small localised works had an even bigger impact because they were progressively worked on by the Fennish for over a thousand years.[14] Eventually it seemed that dykes had existed for so long that they predated human history. According to local mythology, the fen was originally populated by a race of giants whose chief, Hrothgar, had a daughter, Hayenna, who sacrificed two rams to the Water-God to save herself from the unwelcome advances of the Fire Spirit. Hrothgar then had a dream in which he was warned that the Tempest had formed an alliance with the Fire Spirit and that he should prepare for battle by constructing a seven-mile-long deep trench. The Tempest then sent fierce winds that blew down all the trees on the giants, and the Fire Spirit came with a mighty inferno; but Hrothgar, obedient to his dream, tore away the strip of earth separating the newly made dyke from the river, and the thundering water rendered the angry gods powerless. Hrothgar then swore a solemn oath to maintain for all time the rampart between his people and the forest.[15]

Another old legend also emphasises how the wetland protected the Fennish. After the Iceni had become slaves, they rose up and fled following a warning from the god Mandru, that a great flood was coming to sweep away the Romans. A giant wave then swept towards the hills, wiping all before it. After this tsunami (and all the tree trunks preserved in the peat, known as 'bog oaks', *do* face the same way), what had formerly been an impenetrable forest became a vast inland sea whose islands protected the people. Mandru then declared that 'the sea, our great deliverer, shall always be present here, in token whereof ... we shall be known henceforth as Gyrvii or marsh-men, in place of Iceni, the slaves of the Romans'. The Romans did eventually reconquer the country but not even their vigorous draining and skilled road-making could undo the work of the Sea God.[16]

CHAPTER 2

When the Saints Came Marching In: Early Medieval Fenland

The mythology that the Fens were an inhospitable and unpopulated land after the Roman withdrawal from Britain in AD 410 was created by the Church.[1] Accounts of the men and women who founded the region's great monasteries were focused on inspiring piety and pilgrimage, and this required that the saints moved into a harsh and empty wilderness. Nevertheless, there are sufficient clues within even the most fabulous fables to reveal that the new colonisers were not the pioneers penned by the scribes.

The best-known story is that of St Guthlac, the founder of what would become Crowland Abbey. Writing less than 50 years after Guthlac moved to Crowland in AD 699, his biographer and fellow monk, Felix, recorded that what was then an island in the fens had previously been uninhabited because 'no man could endure' its 'manifold horrors and fears, and the loneliness of the wild wilderness'. Apparently this was a 'pestilential' region 'oftimes clouded with moist and dark vapours' whose only residents were the demons who threw Guthlac 'into the muddy waters'.[2] But the *Life of St Guthlac* also documents that the saint was led to Crowland by a local man called Tatwine and made use of *existing* structures for his dwelling: 'There was in the said island a barrow ... in the side of this there appeared to be a kind of tank; in which Guthlac ... began to live, building a shanty over it.'

Was this ceremonial ground for the Fennish? That the island had spiritual significance would explain the reference to 'devils' and Tatwine's reluctance to sleep there because of them. Across the British Isles, colonising monks often settled on existing sacred sites to demonstrate the power of the new religion over the old.

Felix also reveals that for a man living in a supposedly inaccessible wilderness, Guthlac had a remarkable number of visitors and no shortage of helpers to look after him.[3] The reason Guthlac was so successful in his religious pursuits was because he received so much practical support. While the saint battled with devilish visions (probably exaggerated by malarial fever), knowledgeable locals got on with the job of providing him and his fellow-monks with food, shelter and clothing in their time-honoured ways.

Why did the Fennish support Guthlac? The resilience of Celtic Christianity in the British Isles after the Roman departure means that some locals might have already been Christian, so that the monk was not so much converting the people as providing them with resources, including a church. The warm reception St Guthlac received also reflected his family and political status. Guthlac was a noble relative of the Anglo-Saxon King Ethelbald, and the monarch soon became a regular visitor to Crowland. For the Fennish, the holy wanderer was therefore a representative of the royal house of Mercia, both claiming the right of protection and having the capacity to provide it. After Guthlac died, the King gave the island rent-free to his heirs and successors and encouraged a town to be built next to the monastery. Thus, the foundation of the eighth-century monastery seems to have arisen from what was effectively a treaty between the Saxons and the Fennish in which the continued rights of the people to access and control their land was recognised. For Ethelbald, the establishment of the monastery not only won him favour with God but extended the power of his kingdom through integrating the resource-rich Fens and its fiercely independent people into his kingdom's legal, political and religious order.

This pattern of well-connected ecclesiastical colonisation was repeated elsewhere. Ely, which by the tenth century would be the second wealthiest abbey in England, was founded by Etheldreda, the daughter of the King of East Anglia, in AD 673. Although the flight of the princess into the marsh was reputedly undertaken to maintain her chastity (Etheldreda is said to have remained a virgin despite being married off twice for political purposes), her success was undoubtedly helped by having royal status. The fact that Ely was a double monastery, consisting of both nuns and monks under the authority of a woman, shows the continued influence of the indigenous Christianity that evolved in the British Isles during the centuries of comparative isolation after the withdrawal of the Roman legions. A woman, no matter how high in the earthly realm, could not rule over monks in the Roman-governed Church.

St Botolph was another religious leader who founded a monastery with the sanction of a king. Around the community he established in 654 grew Botolph's Ton, eventually shortened to Boston. There were other important religious foundations established at Peterborough (c. 657), Thorney (662) and then Chatteris, Denny, Ramsey, Kyme, Bardney, Spalding and Sempringham. A succession of monarchs and lords granted abbeys large areas of land: both to prove their piety and to extend control over independent areas of their realm. Border tensions between Northumbria, Mercia and East Anglia further fostered royal support for ecclesiastical colonisation. In the Domesday Book, the Abbey of Ramsey is recorded as being the single largest landowner in the nation, owning sixteen manors outright and portions of eight more.[4]

Village-building on the higher islands scattered throughout the Fens was encouraged as part of this process. New Anglo-Saxon settlements included Whaplode, the 'eel-pout stream', Holbeach, 'the deep river', Fleet, 'the tidal stream', and Gedney, 'Gydda's island'. The Spaldas, from which Spalding derived its name, appear in the Tribal Hidage (a list of Saxon tribes) of the seventh century – the name means 'the dwellers by the gulf'. Quadring is the settlement of the 'Haeferingas dwelling in the mud'.[5]

Royal patronage and local support does not mean that the risks and achievements of the saintly pioneers were not real. But monastic vulnerability dramatically declined as the abbeys grew into powerful religious houses under the authority of Rome. Once the abbots effectively became lords of manors, their relations with commoners could be typically medieval and exploitative. An old fen rhyme recalls that some were known to be more oppressive than others:

> Ramsey, the rich of gold and of fee,
> Thorney, the flower of many fair tree;
> Crowland, the courteous, of their meat and their drink,
> Spalding, the gluttons, as all men do think;
> Peterborough, the Proud, as all men do say,
> Sawtrey, by the way – that old Abbey
> Gave more alms in one day – than all they.

Abbeys were places of emergency shelter, philanthropy and hospitality but the abbots could be hard masters and the monks a threat to the poor, particularly vulnerable women.[6]

However, the limits of ecclesiastical oversight and the geographical reality of the marsh ensured that the Fennish preserved an unusual level of economic and cultural independence throughout the feudal period. Over time, a reciprocal relationship developed between the monasteries and local communities which contributed to the resilience of indigenous culture. Tens of thousands of eels and game birds were provided in rents, tithes and sales to monastic houses with little impact on local supply. The men and women who spent much of the day in prayer were fed, sheltered and kept warm with the natural abundance of the fen. Nor were religious houses just the abodes of monks and nuns. Lay brothers and sisters, labourers and servants, provided a further market for food and resources. The size, reliability and nature of this demand, and the distribution of wealth it facilitated, was the foundation for the medieval prosperity of the Fens.

Hugh Candidus described the wealth surrounding his monastery in Peterborough:

> the region of Gyrwas [the Fens] ... begins there on the eastern side, extending for sixty miles or more. The same is very valuable to me because there are obtained there in abundance all things needful for them that dwell nearby, logs and stubble for kindling, hay for the feeding of their beasts, thatch for the roofing of their houses, and many other things of use and profit, and moreover it is very full of fish and fowl. There are diverse rivers and many other waters there, and moreover great fishponds. In all these things that district is very rich. So this [Abbey] is built in a fair spot ...[7]

The downside of prosperity was that, from the late ninth century, it encouraged Viking raids. But the Danes, who achieved effective sovereignty over much of East Anglia, were also reluctant to fight in the marsh, and generally sought to pacify the Fens. King Canute and Queen Emma, early eleventh-century English monarchs who were also rulers of

Denmark and northern lands, are reputed to have been particularly generous to the Fennish. In *Liber Eliensis* (Book of
Ely), it was reported that:

> King Canute gave command by Turkhill the Dane that to
> every village standing about the Fens there should be set out
> a several marsh. Who so divided the ground that each village
> should have so much of the marsh as of the firm ground ...
> And he ordained that the pasture in the marsh should lie
> common for the preservation of peace among them.[8]

Canute is said to have had a favourite hunting lodge at Bodsey
near Ramsey that he would reach by sailing across Whittlesey
Mere (two of his sons are reputed to have drowned in the lake
while crossing it to attend school at Peterborough Abbey).

The Fennish survived the Viking conquest, as they had
that of the Romans and Saxons, through a combination of
direct resistance, accommodating newcomers, adapting to
their presence, and deal-making. But the protection afforded
by the fen would soon be put to its greatest test yet by the
Norman invasion of their wetland home.

CHAPTER 3

The Medieval Fen

The Norman invaders of the Fens, like newcomers before them, soon found themselves stuck in the mud. The cavalry, which was the Normans' main advantage in battle, was effectively neutralised in the swamp, and even movement on foot was difficult without local knowledge. As one nineteenth-century historian observed: 'The Saxons had here the same advantage that the Guerrilla has in his mountains. While they traversed the meres and rivers in small vessels, or ferried in flat-bottomed boats the overflowed shallows, the Normans dare not set foot on the treacherous soil.' The natives 'commenced a harassing warfare … which the Normans called piracy and robbery'.[1]

When victory finally came to William the Conqueror in 1071 it was not the result of military might but a monk's betrayal. The invaders circling Ely were lured into the marsh and the rushes were then set on fire, causing panic in the

Norman ranks. But Abbot Thurstan showed William's soldiers a secret path through the fen, thereby securing both English defeat and Ely's privileges.

William claimed ownership of all of England and parcelled out manors to favoured lords. However, the Norman understanding of land ownership was still far from the modern one. It is sometimes said that all the common land in England was owned by someone after the Norman invasion, with the 'common' referring only to the rights granted to designated villagers to use certain lands for grazing, fishing, hunting, peat collection, hay-making and so on. While this is true, it does not convey the extent to which an acceptance of ordinary people's connection to their ancestral home remained inherent to the medieval notion of property.[2] The common was not a concession or compromise granted by the lords of the manor, but was integral to a world-view in which it was taken for granted that a person *belonged* to the place they came from. This consciousness was underpinned by the fact that without sustenance from the common land, the feudal order of reciprocal obligations could not function and the lords could not receive their due of men and goods. Despite being often codified by Norman rule, the late medieval commons remained a local expression of customs and relationships embedded in country. No place revealed the continuity of customary use more clearly than the Fens.

Most of the Fens remained common land after the conquest, managed and utilised according to traditional practice. In part this was due to the environmental factors which made imposing change difficult. Even those compiling the Domesday Book on behalf of the conquerors did not venture far in the marsh. There are almost no Norman village names in the Fens.[3]

The commons were further protected by the fact that the power of the Fens' existing lords, the monastic abbots, was confirmed by the conquest. As co-dependent beneficiaries of wetland resources, monasteries generally supported the status quo. Unchanged covenants, such as the eel rent paid by commoners of Hilgay and Southery to the Abbey of Bury St Edmunds, show 'the survival of pre-conquest conditions'.[4]

However, the growing power of the Church under Norman patronage also posed a risk to Fennish communities. In the decades following the betrayal at Ely, many new religious houses were established. On the banks of the River Witham alone, there were twelve monastic houses within twenty miles of each other. Ely's own estate expanded considerably in Cambridgeshire and Norfolk.[5] The monasteries' physical presence reached further into the Fens through subsidiary priories, hermitages and shrines. Nunneries, such as 'Crabhouse' and 'Catsholme' in Methwold Fen were also scattered through the countryside.[6] The sites of all these establishments were as much strategic as spiritual. Bridge crossings, causeways, springs and pilgrim roads became places of prayer, profit and power.

Common land could be threatened by this expansion. It is recorded in the archives of Crowland that during the summer of 1189, 'the men of Holland,* who are our neighbours on the northern side, strongly desire[d] to have common of the marsh of Crowland', and occupied the pastures being claimed by the monastery. Three thousand commoners asserted their claim, refusing to remove their animals despite the abbot's bailiffs impounding as many as they could. Not even one of the wealthiest abbeys in all England proved able to defeat such a united opposition.[7]

One of the new religious settlements initiated during this period (the only uniquely English religious order ever established) was Fennish in its foundation. In the early twelfth century, Gilbert of Sempringham gave up some of his estate to establish a nunnery at the request of a group of local village women. It was only because the Church required that nuns be overseen by a priest that Gilbert subsequently founded an order of canons – communities of active priests living together under a common rule near the enclosed nunneries. The patriarchal structure facilitated Rome's sanction but Gilbert's unwavering commitment to a modified expression of the Celtic mixed-gender monastery still invoked Papal distrust. Gilbert resisted geographically separating men and women, and the King, who saw advantages in having a native English religious order, supported the fenman's stand.[8]

---

* Lincolnshire was historically divided into three administrative districts – Holland, Lindsey and Kesteven. Most of Holland and much of Lindsey was fenland.

One of these royal benefits became evident when Sempringham Abbey was used to confine the last Welsh princess. Princess Gwenllian (1282–1337) was the only child of the Prince of Wales who was murdered on the orders of King Edward I when his daughter was six months old. The infant heir to the Welsh throne was abducted and confined to the Gilbertine nunnery where she would spend the rest of her life – probably grateful to have escaped even more violent political intrigue.

Monastic expansion created tensions but also provided economic opportunities for the local people. Growing demand for the products of the fen largely explains why during the thirteenth and fourteenth centuries the Fennish became some of the best-off commoners in England. In 1334, the Lay Subsidy or tax assessment per acre of the Lincolnshire fenland was the fourth highest in the kingdom, with the seaward fens containing 31 of the 106 richest places in England.[9] The inland marshland was also remarkably prosperous: as its legacy of magnificent churches reveals.

The medieval prosperity of the Fens meant a renewed appreciation of its bounty and beauty. In the thirteenth century, Henry of Huntingdon described 'this fenny country' as 'very pleasant and agreeable to the eye, watered by many rivers which run through it, diversified with many large and small lakes and adorned with many roads and islands'. William of Malmesbury depicted the wetland as 'a very paradise and a heaven for the beauty and delight thereof, the very marshes bearing goodly trees', with such an 'abundance of fish as to cause astonishment to strangers, while natives laugh at their surprise. Water-fowl are so plentiful that persons may not assuage their hunger with both sorts of food but eat to satisfy for a penny.'[10]

This was the period when sea fishing for cod, haddock and herring became established on a large scale. The harvesting of shellfish also increased, especially of oysters but also other species such as mussels and whelks.[11] There was, in addition, more intensive exploitation of freshwater fish. The chronicler of Ramsey Abbey wrote of Ramsey Mere that in its depths 'there are frequently taken, with several kinds of nets, as well as with baited hooks, and other fishing instruments, pike of extraordinary great size, called *hakedes* by the country folk: and though both fishers and fowlers cease neither by day nor night to frequent it, yet there is always no little store of fish.'[12]

Eels were so plentiful and widely consumed that they sometimes served as a de facto currency. Rents and tithes could be defined in terms of thousands of eels or in 'sticks' of 25.[13] The twelfth-century villages of Doddington, Littleport and Stuntney alone contributed 68,000 eels a year to the abbot-bishop of Ely.[14]

However, the most valuable resource of all was grass. A shortage of feed in high summer was a continual problem in the open fields of the Middle Ages but no such paucity afflicted the Fens. The annual winter flooding deposited a rich layer of silt which fertilised the lush summer meadows.

Just as important to economic prosperity was the comparatively equal distribution of wealth afforded by the vast common. Joan Thirsk documented how the Fenland differed from other regions in having 'a higher proportion of small farmers and a lower proportion of very wealthy ones'. Instead of the enormous divisions in wealth which characterised the arable regions of England, there was 'a series of regular gradations from the top downwards' and a distinctly large group of 'middling-rich yeomen'.[15] The region also had landless people but the size and wealth of the commons ensured that even these folk were generally able to own some livestock, sell marketable products and make a productive contribution to communal life.

The medieval prosperity of the Fens thus occurred not *in spite* of the survival of a vast undrained marshland but *because* of it. The fact that comparatively high living standards were sustained despite increased demands being made upon the environment is a testament to the skill with which the land was managed. There is no complete record of customary management systems but court records provide a glimpse of some of the rules that ensured sustainable resource use. In 1304 Aylward le Turnere was expelled from the manor of Ramsey 'for waste of the fen'. John Bantelig and John Herring were both presented at the manor court at Littleport, the former for mowing sedge 'before the feast of St John against the general ordinance', the latter for employing 'two men mowing in the fen where he should have but one'. Guy Bullok was charged with having 'on 1 February 1396, by force of arms narrowed the common river of Holbeach ... to the damage of the whole community'. Thomas Halmere, Simon Malle and John Hare were prosecuted because they 'by force of arms and with dogs' impeded the common 'sewer'* in Weston 'with nets and other fishing contrivances'.[16]

Most community policing centred on the grasslands, which were managed through ancient 'intercommoning' arrangements across different parishes. Each year there were great musters or 'drifts', during which all the animals grazing on the common were counted: with those not belonging to rightful commoners being impounded and released only on the payment of a fine. By the late Middle Ages, the precise boundaries of the commons were being defined, with fierce border disputes not unknown.[17]

Sustainable land management did not preclude some drainage works. The Bishop of Ely, John Morton, turned the River Nene north of Whittlesey into a ten-mile-long canal known as 'Morton's Leam' during the late fifteenth century in an attempt to redirect the Nene back through Wisbech (the port town had lost access to the sea after the river, choked with silt, had changed its course towards King's Lynn).[18] The Witham, Welland and Great Ouse rivers were also straightened to improve drainage and navigation, and a new canal was dug through a narrow neck of land to link the Nene and Old Croft rivers.[19] Even some of the commoner-initiated schemes were quite large – residents of Holland Fen near Boston maintained

---

* A 'sewer' was an artificial watercourse that was associated with draining land.

a twenty-mile bank.[20] Most drainage, however, was small-scale, even if the long-term impact of sustained digging could be considerable. Loosely nucleated villages located on the slightly higher silt lands were commonly at the head of a long, narrow parish that extended from the coast into the lower-lying back fen, and as population increased, areas of both salt and freshwater wetland could be slowly drained. Over time, farms often spread down a series of linear drove-ways that linked the villages with the common pasture.[21]

Monasteries and commoners could also work together to increase the area of farming land. By 1330, Goll Grange, established by Spalding Abbey on land that it protected from flooding, comprised 292 acres of arable ground and 195 acres of meadow.[22] Areas of salt marsh were reclaimed from the sea through similar partnerships but none of this activity substantially impacted on the vast wetland common.

Rising sea levels from the fourteenth century posed a significant new challenge. The origins of the sea wall that protected much of medieval Fenland are not clear and it is likely that its construction was not a single event, but by the late Middle Ages there was a continuous barrier to the sea from King's Lynn through Wisbech to Spalding.[23]

These defences could not prevent the occasional disaster. *Stowe's Chronicle* records that on New Year's Day 1287:

As well through the vehemence of the wind as the violence of the sea, the monasteries of Spalding and many churches were overthrown and destroyed. The whole of Holland, in

Lincolnshire, was, for the most part, turned into a standing pool; so that an intolerable multitude of men, women and children were overwhelmed with the water, especially the town of Boston, or Buttolph's Town, a great part of whereof was destroyed.[24]

In 1467 it was recorded that there 'was so great an inundation of the waters, by reason of the snows and continuous rains that no man then living could recall to mind the like. Throughout the whole of South Holland there was scarce a house or building but what the waters made their way and flowed in; and this remained continuously during a whole month.'[25]

Disputes about who was responsible for maintaining flood protection infrastructure were commonplace. It was partly in order to establish legal mechanisms to resolve such disputes that Commissions of Sewers were established. These were initially temporary quasi-legal bodies designed to respond to immediate problems. The first was set up in Lincolnshire by the aptly named Henry de Bathe in 1258. The powers of subsequent courts were gradually reinforced by legislation until Henry VIII's Statute of Sewers codified their permanent judicial, executive and legislative powers, including the right of commissioners to levy taxes and order works to be undertaken. The Commissions represented the first significant interference by the national government in the management of the Fens. Nevertheless, during the medieval period, the commissioners were not so much seeking to implement new rules as to effectively enforce the existing ones.

Management was still done locally using commoner expertise. The system needed to be responsive to local conditions because this was a land where coast, creeks and rivers could markedly shift within one lifetime. Areas might silt up, flood and just as rapidly return from the sea; even the tide was not always predictable. The cultural practices of the Fennish, like those of other indigenous cultures, were closely attuned to the ever-altering environment, with each generation of inhabitants adapting to the evolving landscape. The nature of their home ensured that the Fennish were a people inherently open to change.

CHAPTER 4

Reformation to Reclamation: 1530–1630

The dissolution of the monasteries in the 1530s by King Henry VIII led to the most radical change in land ownership since the Norman conquest, and in no part of England was the impact greater than the Fens. Those who purchased or were bequeathed the vast monastic holdings often had no ties to the local community or regard for customary practice, let alone a willingness to receive their rents in eels, fish and game birds.[1] Tyndale's 1528 prayer that 'Christian landlords' would 'be content with their rent and old customs' and 'not take in their commons' because 'God gave the earth to man to inhabit, and not unto sheep and deer' was medieval nostalgia to many of the nouveaux-riches.[2]

Landowners across England took advantage of the economic, social and religious flux associated with the Reformation to enclose land. Although the process of enclosure varied greatly, the outcome could be ruthless – aerial photography and excavations have located more than a thousand English villages that were deserted during the sixteenth century: many razed for parks and pasture. As Sir Thomas More observed in *Utopia*, 'they pluck down townes and leave nothing standing, but only the church to be made a sheep house'.[3]

For some commoners, dispossession from their ancestral country meant dependence on the vagaries of wage labour; for others it brought destitution – by the end of the sixteenth century there were twelve times the number of landless people as a hundred years before. New laws targeted vagrants as medieval systems of charity, which had been built around the monastic houses and other institutions of the Church, broke down.[4] To curb unrest and fill some of the welfare gap, the new poor laws enacted in 1598 and 1601 made parishes responsible for relief of their own, but heaven help the homeless stranger for whom poverty had become a crime.

Expropriation did not come without resistance. In 1549, 16,000 people gathered at a common on the outskirts of Norwich known as Mousehold Heath, where they formed a makeshift government under the leadership of Robert Kett. After marching into the city the resistance was forcibly put down with the aid of German mercenaries, but their 'camping time' was immortalised in popular memory. The first of the 29 articles that made up the manifesto of the rebellion was 'We pray ... from henceforth no man shall enclose any more'; the third was a prayer 'that no lord of no manor shall common upon the Commons'.[5]

Enclosure was a particularly potent threat to the Fennish because the dissolution of the monasteries coincided with improved drainage technology, population growth, a shortage of land in other regions, and a growing demand for fen resources.[6] Increasing numbers of dispossessed people also moved to villages with commons rights – a movement that increased economic growth but also posed environmental challenges.[7]

Another serious threat to the sustainability of the commons was the growing temptation to bring in stock for the sole purpose of fattening them for sale to the expanding London market.[8] Commoners testified in the Court of Exchequer that the practice of bringing in outside cattle originated in about 1548 and had no precedent. In 1575 John Chetham of Frampton Manor near Boston, who had agreed to graze 200 'northern cattle' in the fen for five years running, withdrew them after protests by commoners. In 1580, the fen 'graves' appointed to oversee the common pastures at Frampton drove out 160 sheep belonging to Thomas Cholmeley of Burton Coggles. A range of solutions were found to settle disputes, including setting a maximum number of 200 sheep that any one person could place on the common, excluding children and servants in the allocation, and restricting geese herds to 60.[9]

Problems also emerged with the maintenance of drainage works after the dissolution of the monasteries. In 1575 a complaint was made to Queen Elizabeth I concerning the lack of upkeep of Brigdyke, the causeway between Boston and Kesteven. Its maintenance had long been charged to

Sempringham Abbey, which had established a priory at Bridge
End near Horbling with specific responsibility for the ancient
road across the marsh.[10] However, the engineering problems
of the sixteenth century should not be exaggerated (something
later drainage apologists were wont to do). The simple truth
is that ordinary people of the Fens, not the monks or their
servants, had always undertaken most maintenance work, and
this they continued to do.[11]

The bigger story of the sixteenth century was the capacity of commoners to successfully adapt to the challenges
posed by the post-Reformation world. Joan Thirsk's research
on the Fens confirmed that 'no significant change took place
in the numbers of stock held by the average farmer between
1530 and the end of the century. An ordinary farm carried
some ten cattle, six horses, four pigs, and about twenty sheep.'
The wealthiest farmer in her sample was William Somerby of
Horbling who had 25 head, with the average farmer having
from five to seventeen animals. By European peasant norms
these were large numbers, and directly reflected the wealth of
the common pastures. One in every two inventories collected
in the 1560s and 1590s also referred to 'pullen' (meaning geese,
hens, ducks and capons) that also spent time in the communal marsh. Thirsk observed that 'there were many more of
the poorer sort' of people not represented in the inventories.
These folk 'kept some sheep and a cow or two and fed them
on the commons'.[12]

The sheer size of the wetland seems to have helped the
Fennish adapt to the emerging market economy. While the

median land holding was only about four acres, these small farms were not as vulnerable to market-driven rationalisation as they were elsewhere in England because of the extensive common pastures.[13]

The higher prices for fish and game caused by increasing population and the rapid growth of London during the sixteenth century provided further opportunities for the entrepreneurial Fennish. It is a testament to the skill and expertise with which the common was still being managed that increased demand led to stricter controls over supply. From 1534, the wildfowling season was closed between May and August in the Cambridgeshire fen. At Epworth in the Isle of Axholme, the right 'to set bush nets and catch white fish' was restricted to Wednesdays and Fridays. The stocking of many fen pastures was not allowed earlier than May Day.[14]

The most famous regulatory reform package was the 72 articles of the 1548 'Fen Charter'. This code would define management of the commons of southern Lincolnshire for more than 250 years. It set out that no 'foreigners' could use the fen, with each parish being given its own brand so that cattle could be identified. Penalties were incurred for a vast range of offences including the introduction of diseased animals, allowing dogs to disturb cattle or roam after sunset, and leaving dead animals unburied. Regulations guided the driving of cattle, the mowing of fodder and the hunting of wild birds (no moulted ducks to be taken before midsummer day).[15] No reed was to be mown for thatch before it had two years' growth; and no swans', cranes', or bitterns' eggs could be taken from the fen at all. Dates were set for the use of natural resources and permitted technology was prescribed.[16]

A related code of seventeen articles was drawn up by a fishermen's jury which regulated the type of nets that were allowed and how they were to be used.[17] A similarly detailed body of regulations was set out relating to the management and farming of swans.[18]

The value placed on the Charter was expressed by an old Fennish rhyme:

> Maiden's garter, fenman's charter,
> Neighbours' brats, fishermen's floats,
> Fire a'glowing, reaper mowing,
> Are things never interfered with.[19]

This body of regulation to manage the common was an innovative response by customary land managers to the challenges posed by a post-monastic, increasingly market-driven economy. The reforms seem to have been a success: maintaining equitable access to resources while preventing over-exploitation by the rich newcomers who now held title to monastic estates. Michael Drayton's *Polyolbion* (1622) gives a glimpse of the continued wealth of the undrained wetland:

> The toyling Fisher here is tewing of his Net:
> The Fowler is imployd his lymed twigs to set.
> One underneath his Horse, to get a shoot doth stalke;
> Another over Dykes upon his Stilts doth walke:

> There other with their Spades, the Peats are squaring out,
> And others from their Carres, are busily about
> To draw out Sedge and Reed, for Thatch and Stover fit.[20]

Nevertheless, despite or because of the evident economic prosperity, the determination of some landowners to enclose their lands intensified as the sixteenth century progressed. In the Netherlands, over 100,000 acres of marsh were reclaimed from 1565 to 1615, and the Dutch quickly became the principal contractors for even more ambitious drainage projects in northern Germany and other European countries. However, no Fen drainage scheme progressed far until 1589 when (with the critical support of Lord Burghley – Queen Elizabeth's closest adviser) an Anglo-Dutchman, Humphrey Bradley, outlined a plan to drain an area 70 miles by 30 miles in size.[21] This project was presented to the monarch in classic imperial terms:

> Given that the lands are freed from the superfluous water, there remains to be described a vast number of benefits and advantages that would accrue to the Crown ... the change will be so striking that it could not be greater in a work of this kind; a vague, deserted Empire without population turned into a fertile region; and wild and useless products therefrom into an abundance of grain and pasturage; humble huts into a beautiful and opulent city, together with various other benefits. With good regulation, the drained land will be a regal conquest, a new republic and complete state.[22]

The Queen rejected this drainage plan but in 1598, a scheme promoted by the influential Sir John Popham, variously Lord Chief Justice, member of the Privy Council, Speaker of the House of Commons and investor in colonisation projects from Ireland to Virginia, won her support.[23] In 1601, Elizabeth signed into law an Act for 'the recovering of many hundred thousand Acres of marshes, and other Grounds ... within the Isle of Ely, and in the Counties of Cambridge, Huntingdon, Northampton, Lincoln, Norfolk, Suffolk, Sussex, Essex, Kent and the County Palatine of Durham'.[24]

The 1601 General Drainage Act required only that a majority of commoners consent to enclosure and ensured that those who undertook and invested in the work would be entitled to a share of the land.[25] The preamble of the Act did concede 'that anything herein contained shall not extend to the impairing, diminishing, letting, taking away, or extinguishing of the interests of the commoners', but rights could be bought out and many customary users proved to have no common 'right' at all.[26]

The passage of the Act encouraged Popham and his partners, including the entrepreneurial engineer Thomas Lovell (who had successfully patented new drainage techniques learnt during military service in the Netherlands), to pursue their dream of draining much of the southern fens – until being stalled by the unexpected strength of the resistance. As Eric Ash has documented: 'Hundreds of commoners protested to the commission of sewers, petitioned both Crown and Parliament ... and hampered the construction works.'[27] Thomas Wells of Deeping St James, described as a day labourer, was singled out by a prosecuting court. Wells was reported to have harangued the parishioners in his local church at the end of the service on 1 April 1603 to fill in the enclosure ditches and kill anyone in their way. On 5 April, at least sixteen commoners began to level the ditches and expel Lovell's workmen, threatening to bury Lovell himself in one of his ditches and cripple any workman who returned. Wells petitioned the new King James I not to allow the commons to be taken from him and his poor neighbours, but the royal proclamation only condemned the disturbances. However, the limits of the monarch's power became evident when his orders were ignored by local officials sympathetic to the commoners (whose cause was further aided by floods and dubious engineering).[28]

Four further legislative attempts – in 1606, 1607, 1610, and 1621 – to get legal backing for drainage schemes failed to overcome parliamentary opposition despite active support from King James. Others continued to be defeated through direct action. One evening in June 1619, about 2,000 of what was described as the 'common sort of people' gathered to oppose a drainage scheme proposed by the Court of Sewers – the protesters rang bells, banged drums and discharged muskets around bonfires for much of the night.[29]

About 4,000 acres of fenland in the Isle of Ely were successfully drained and enclosed in 1624 through a deal struck with the Dean and Chapter of Ely Cathedral (heirs of some of the monastic estate). However, such was the resistance to the appropriation of the common that Parliament received a petition on this matter as late as 1645, and seven commoners (all of them Parliamentary soldiers) were committed to gaol that year for continuing to fight it.[30]

An attempt to survey and partition the Cambridgeshire fens at Soham in 1629 also provoked fierce resistance. When the Exchequer commissioners attended the manor court to read out the order dividing the commons, a crowd of 200–300 people, mainly comprising women, threw stones at the commissioners who had to take refuge in a nearby house. Those laying siege vowed they 'would tear the commissioners and whomsoever else had any hand in this business'. In another incident at nearby Chippenham, it was the workers on the scheme who sabotaged it 'by flinging in the earth which they were paid … to fling out'.[31]

Opponents of enclosure and drainage emphasised the ethical issues that were at stake. In 1597–98, Lord Willoughby had pointed out that some fens 'lye onely surrouwnded with water in winter, which in sommor ar excellent pasture and yeelde great profit'. This benevolent aristocrat noted that if these lands were included in a drainage scheme, 'instead of helping the gennerall pore, it would undo them and make those that are allreddye ritch farr more ritch'.[32]

Another philosophical critic of drainage proposals in the early 1620s wrote that large-scale engineering works were against the will of God, since 'fens were made fens and must ever continue such'. Using a similar argument, William Camden argued in *Britannia* that: 'As touching the drying up of this Fenny country … So many think it the wisest and best course according to the sage admonition in like case of *Apollo* [in] his Oracle, *Not to intermeddle at all with that which God hath ordeined*.'[33]

The main source of political support for drainage came from the cash-hungry Stuart kings. In 1620, King James declared that 'for the honour of his kingdom' he 'would not long suffer these countries to be abandoned to the will of the waters' nor 'let them lie waste and unprofitable', and would personally undertake drainage around Hatfield Chase in the northern Fenland in return for 120,000 acres of the enclosed land. The great advantage of choosing this wetland was that while the commons were extensive, the King was the lord of the manor, and the estate included the only significant royal 'forest' (as lands exclusively set aside for hunting were termed) in the Fens.[34] James died in 1625 before his plans were put into action but four years later King Charles I would resurrect his father's dream.[35]

Around the same time in the southern Fenland, a group of frustrated landowners approached the mega-wealthy and politically powerful Francis Russell, Earl of Bedford, the owner of a large estate near Thorney and Whittlesey, with yet another drainage proposal. The Earl agreed to drain a vast expanse of marsh and in 1631 thirteen 'Adventurers' associated themselves with the project (an Adventurer was one who 'adventured' his capital in the enterprise, while 'Undertaker' was the term adopted for those who 'undertook' to do the work of drainage). In 1634 the Bedford Level Corporation was granted a charter by which 'it was hoped in those places which lately presented nothing to the eyes of the beholder, but great waters and a few reeds scattered here and there, under Divine mercy might be seen pleasant pastures of cattle and kyne and many houses belonging to their inhabitants'.[36]

One of the new class of entrepreneurial Dutch engineers who were then selling their drainage expertise across Europe, Cornelius Vermuyden, was contracted to develop the project.[37] Vermuyden's scheme involved cutting a new straight water course called the Bedford River (now the Old Bedford River) that was to be 21 miles long and 70 feet wide, as well as another smaller canal.[38]

Resistance to the proposed drainage was immediate but this time the proponents were not backing down. The phoney war was over; the fight for the Fens had begun.

CHAPTER 5

The Fight for the Great Level

The commencement of work on the Bedford Corporation's project to drain the more than 300,000 acres of marsh in the southern fens known as the 'Great Level' provoked immediate resistance. The ballad, 'Powtes Complaint' was a call to arms:

> Come, Brethren of the water, and let us all assemble,
> To treat upon this matter, which makes us quake and
>   tremble;
> For we shall rue it, if't be true, that Fens be undertaken,
> And where we feed in Fen and Reed, they'll feed both
>   Beef and Bacon.
> Away with boats and rudder, farewell both boots and
>   skatches,
> No need of one nor th'other, men now make better
>   matches;
> Stilt-makers all and tanners, shall complain of this disaster,

For they will make each muddy lake for Essex calves a
    pasture.
The feather'd fowls have wings, to fly to other nations;
But we have no such things, to help our transportations;
We must give place (oh grievous case) to horned beasts and
    cattle,
Except that we can all agree to drive them out by battle.[1]

The first documented casualty of the conflict occurred in 1628 when a commoner was killed by one of the Dutch drainage workers embroiled in conflict with the local people.[2] Resistance was not confined to the southern fens. A lawsuit in April 1629 described how the villagers of Torksey, near Lincoln:

> came unto the workmen and beat and terrified them, threatening to kill them, if they would not leave their work, threw some of them into the river and kept them under water with long poles, and at several other times, upon the Knelling of a Bell, came to the said works in riotous and warlike manner, divided themselves into companies, to take the workmen and filled up the ditches and drains, made to carry away the water, burned up the working tools and other materials of the Relator and his workmen, and set up poles in the form of gallows, to terrifie the workmen and threatened to break their arms and legs, and beat and hurt many of them and made others flee away, whom they pursued to a town with such terror and threats, that they were forced to guard the town.[3]

The situation in Soham, whose residents were resisting the drainage and enclosure of their 10,000-acre common marsh, came before the Privy Council in May 1632, seemingly as a test case to establish a precedent for the severe punishment of commoners. However, the main effect of the action was to reveal how difficult it was to enforce central authority.

The constables charged with arresting the four Soham resistance leaders so delayed entering the village that they were later charged for not putting the warrant into effect. When they finally sought to do so, an estimated 200 people poured onto the streets armed with forks, staves and stones. The next day a justice ordered 60 men to support the constables in executing the warrant but over 100 townspeople still stood defiant, warning 'that if any laid hands of any of them, they would kill or be killed'. When one of the four was finally arrested, the constables were attacked and several people were injured. A justice arrived in Soham on 11 June with about 120 men and made a further arrest before the justice's men were again 'beaten off, the rest never offering to aid them'. Another of the four leaders, Anne Dobbs, was eventually caught and imprisoned in Cambridge Castle but on 14 June 1633, the fight was resumed when about 70 people filled in six division ditches meant to form part of an enclosure. Twenty offenders were identified, of whom fourteen were women.[4]

When the drainage works of the Great Level were (prematurely) deemed complete in 1636 and enclosure began in earnest, protests accelerated with bridges, roads and other works destroyed. Justices sent up from London reported that 'disordered and Mutinous persons in sundry parts of the great Level of the fens have taken Encouragement to disturb and interrupt the workmen'.[5]

In the early spring of 1637, the commoners of Upwell in Norfolk rose and 'mutinously disturbed' the works. The Privy Council ordered the arrest of nineteen people, including two seemingly disloyal constables, but the fight spread to Cambridgeshire in May. The woman described as 'the first mover of this mutiny' was condemned as a 'witch' who used 'magic' against the Undertakers' workers, before being sent to Wisbech prison. The commons shared by the inhabitants of Wretton, Stoke Ferry and Dereham in Norfolk were the scene of further clashes in May 1637. The people claimed they were engaged in their customary annual procession around the boundary of the fens when they came across workmen in a spot where they usually caught wildfowl.

The King decisively backed the Undertakers at a Privy Council meeting on 11 July 1637, promising immediate assistance to any Adventurer, and dismissing all the complaints made to him about the enclosure except those from the representatives of Ely Cathedral and Cambridge colleges (which were referred to the surveyor general).[6] Local justices of the peace were given clear instructions: 'Suppress these tumults.'[7]

But even a royal order was difficult to implement in the fen villages. The dangers facing the 'messengers' of His Majesty were serious. Two men charged with arresting protesters at Wicken near Soham reported that when they met with the local constable, he warned them not to enter the village and discoursed 'against the draining and the taking in of the Fens'. When the warning was ignored, people came out with pitch-forks and poles, and gathered around a place where great heaps of stones were laid. After an attempt was made to arrest the resistance leader, John Moreclark, he reportedly proclaimed that 'he would obey no Warrant from any Lords', and even after being informed 'that it was a Warrant from a Secretary of State by his Majesty's special command … answered again that he would obey no Warrant at all from anyone whatso-ever'. As Moreclark pushed back with his pike, 'the women got together to [throw] the heaps of stones at the messengers, who were scoffed at and abused by the whole multitude'. The King's men were powerless to act, given the crowd's expressed resolution that 'if anyone were taken away, they would all be taken', and were forced to ride out of town to the jeers of the victorious villagers.[8]

The popular curate of Wicken, who was both a local justice and landowner, seems to have provided support to the villagers. A constable testified that when several rioters were brought before the cleric he did not charge them but instead 'persuaded them that two of them should voluntarily go to prison, promising them that he would see that they should want nothing, and that he would endeavour to get them out of prison'.

Local juries could also be sympathetic to the commoners. After drainage works in other parts of Cambridgeshire were attacked at the end of May 1638 by persons 'of the meaner sort' who were believed to come from Wicken, Burwell, Swaffham

Prior, Swaffham Bulbeck and Bottisham, two local justices and a jury were assembled by the sheriff and an inquiry was held. The jury found 'for want of sufficient evidence and proof' against only one man – Thomas Shipp of Burwell – who was imprisoned in Cambridge Castle. Shipp confessed that he and his six colleagues were part of a larger group that had levelled enclosures in four different localities.[9]

By 1638, it was feared that the Fennish revolt posed a serious threat to national security. On 6 June of that year, the local landowner and Bedford Corporation Undertaker, Sir Miles Sandys of Wilburton, wrote to his son at Court to document the 'great riot made at Wickham [sic] by hurling in my Lord of Bedford's works' and declared that if 'order be not taken, it will turn out to be a general rebellion in all the Fen towns'. Even 'whilst writing', word was brought to Sir Miles that 'the country rose up ... both in Coveney and Littleport, by example of the Wickham men'. At Bottisham too there were 'treasonable speeches'.[10] Sandys suggested that this was intelligence with which his well-placed son would 'do well [to] acquaint the Lords'.[11]

Sandys had heard that the action to protect the common of the people of Ely, Little Downham and Littleport would spread further under the guise of playing football – with the 'first blow at the ball' being the signal to begin levelling. This plan was forestalled by arrests and torrential rain but on 6 June about 200 men filled in enclosure ditches. The action was supported by commoners from as far away as the Suffolk towns of Lakenheath and Mildenhall, and it was clear that coordinated action was now occurring across the region, with London being informed that 'one Town [was] holding privy intelligence with another'.[12]

Four leaders were arrested and put in Ely gaol, but such was the level of local resentment at this that a local justice warned the Privy Council that a 'thousand people' who had become 'desperately careless, and nourish bad spirits amongst themselves' were set 'to rise'. He advised that warrants of arrest were meaningless as they were 'resisted by some, neglected by others, and some that are charged in his Majesty's name to aid the Constables ... refuse it'.[13]

At this stage of the protests, the commoners' target was not the King but the enclosing landowners, with the Fennish still more likely to appeal to the monarch than target him. In 1638, Edward Powell was prosecuted for paying the Ely town crier to assemble townspeople in the marketplace to petition the King (who was spending Lent in Newmarket), 'for the losing of their fens would be the losing of their Livelihoods'. Powell wanted the Crown to intervene against the local justices whom he saw to be in league with the enclosing Bishop of Ely. This action popularised a story that 'the King at Newmarket leaned on his shoulder and wept' on hearing Powell's account of the suffering caused by enclosure. In fact it seems the King's Lenten meditations were uninterrupted, but Powell did tell the court that the Ely justices were 'but the Bishop's Justices and not the King's'. Even after 21 days in Ely gaol, Powell maintained that 'I will not leave my Common until I see the King's own Signet: I will obey God and the

King but no man else.' Powell was given a £200 fine⋆ and imprisoned until May 1639 but had to be moved to London's Newgate prison to prevent the danger of 'further mischief' should he continue to be confined in Ely.[14]

The Earl of Exeter was charged by the King with restoring order and quickly recognised the potential for commoner discontent to help the royal cause. In a letter from Huntingdon on 9 June 1638, he argued that 'Your Majesty shall not need to fear a general revolt', for what was sought was only 'reformation' of the common. The Earl believed the villagers to be otherwise 'dutiful subjects and in the end if upon the suppressing of these tumults, which grow upon the rage the poor people bear to these enclosures, your Majesty show a public reformation by law, the effect will be to your Majesty's great honour to the great contentment of your people and the placing of yourself and posterity in peace and security.'[15]

The old-fashioned aristocrat could see the link between restoring order and protecting traditional rights. However, loyalty to the King was more provisional than he assumed. The Fennish priority was the defence of the commons, and people generally backed any arm of the increasingly divided state that supported them in this.

⋆ There was no prospect of such a fine being paid. Even the minority of full-time agricultural labourers during the seventeenth century were receiving considerably less than £20 per year. Workers in towns generally earned more than this, but a £200 fine represented many years' wages even for the best-paid of them.

Despite the drainage works supposedly being complete, flooding returned to the Great Level in the winter of 1636–37, and some Adventurers appealed to the King for redress. Charles called an investigatory session of the Commission of Sewers which on 12 April 1638 declared that the drainage had not been completed within the agreed six-year period. This finding provided an opportunity for the cash-starved monarch to personally replace the Bedford Corporation as Undertaker, which he did in July 1638 in return for 57,000 acres of drained land. William Dugdale wrote that Charles even intended to transform the village of Manea into the town of 'Charlemont' according to designs the King drew up himself.[16]

However, the same session of the Court of Sewers also granted a concession to the commoners. It was determined that they could retain possession of areas where drainage works were deemed deficient pending adjudication by the Court. With national politics now moving from crisis to conflict, the King had other priorities to pursue, and even functional engineering works fell into neglect. At the same time, appeals and counter-appeals were made by both sides to the houses of Parliament, as the fight in the Fens became intertwined with the power struggle that would culminate in civil war.[17]

CHAPTER 6

Revolutionary Swamps: Civil War in the Fen

Oliver Cromwell came from the Fens; his ancestor Sir Richard Cromwell having purchased a large part of the property of Ramsey Abbey when the monasteries were dissolved. Descendants dissipated their inheritance but at the time of Oliver's birth in Huntingdon in 1599, the Cromwells remained the leading family of the town. In 1636 Oliver inherited the estate and moved with his family to Ely.[1]

Cromwell's ancestral lands were central to the conflict over the drainage and enclosure of the Great Level. In the summer of 1637, the Privy Council was informed that 'a great many women and men' went into Holme Fen near Huntingdon with scythes and pitchforks to 'let out the guts of any one that should drive their fens'. The following year, the Council heard that: 'It was commonly reported … that Mr Cromwell of Ely, had undertaken, they paying him a groat [a silver four penny piece] for every cow they had upon the common, to hold the drainers in suit of law for five years, and that in the meantime they should enjoy every part of their common.'[2] When the King decided to take this project into his own hands, William Dugdale reports that Cromwell was 'especially made choice of by those who ever endeavoured the undermining of regal authority, to be their orator at Huntingdon unto the … King's Commissioners of Sewers there, in opposition to his Majesty's most commendable design'.[3]

Cromwell remained an advocate, adviser and spokesperson for the Fennish as national tensions escalated during 1641, successfully taking the commoner cause to the national stage, and ensuring that a clause concerning the commandeering of common land in the Fens was included in the catalogue of complaints known as the Grand Remonstrance presented to the King that year.[4]

A 1643 petition from commoners affected by the Great Level drainage was referred to a parliamentary committee that included Cromwell. The committee chair, Edward Hyde, later reported that his high-profile colleague 'appeared much concerned to countenance the Petitioners, who were numerous, together with their witnesses' and 'enlarged upon what They said with great Passion'. Hyde saw the commoners as 'a very rude Kind of People' and reported that Cromwell 'in great Fury reproached the Chairman for being partial' and attacked the defence of enclosures 'with so much Indecency, and Rudeness, and in Language, so contrary, and offensive … that the Chairman found himself obliged to reprehend him'.[5]

Such was his identification with the marsh, that in the increasingly violent conflict engulfing the country, Cromwell was derided by his Royalist opponents as 'Lord of the Fens' (that is, Lord of 'nothing').

Given Cromwell's personal history, it might have been expected that his military victory with the Parliamentary forces and ascent to power would be decisive in confirming the commoners' possession of their lands. But unfortunately for the Fennish, the principal Undertakers in the Great Level project also backed the winning side. William, the new Earl of Bedford was a general in the Parliamentary cavalry; while other Adventurers, including Sir Miles Sandys, Francis Underwood and George Glapthorne, actively supported Parliament in Cambridgeshire and Ely.[6] In 1646, these men sought new laws to facilitate the redraining of the Great Level. A committee of pro-drainage MPs charged with progressing this objective reported back to Parliament in March 1648. Cromwell was named as one of the drainage commissioners, together with the Earl of Bedford, in the Act for the Draining of the Great Level. There was enduring controversy about the circumstances in which the Bill was finally passed in May 1649. Opponents alleged that there were only 43 MPs present, and that a number of these had financial interests in the project.[7]

The new legislation was even more pro-enclosure than the old, royally-mandated laws, as the consent of the majority of commoners no longer had to be obtained for drainage works to proceed. A larger principle was now invoked, 'the consent of the Nation', with the national interest seen to override individual, communal and regional objections. Why should 'covetous ... self-seekers' be able to put 'their private interests before the public good?', a drainage apologist asked. To prioritise the rights of commoners was an 'unsound, destructive principle' that could 'interrupt the great affairs of this Commonwealth'.[8]

The Fennish were not without their own influential friends. The most vocal supporters of their cause were the Levellers, a radical and ultimately suppressed wing of the English revolution who sought to extend suffrage and other political rights to common people. Their 11 September 1648 petition to Parliament had 40,000 signatures and among its 27 demands were the opening of 'all late enclosures of Fens and other Commons'.[9] However, the leader most concerned with the Fennish cause, John Lilburne, was prosecuted for treason in 1649 and temporarily exiled in 1651, his defence of the Fennish part of an increasingly suppressed campaign to highlight Cromwell's apparent abandonment of many of those he once stood with.[10]

The most gifted apologist for the Fennish cause was the lawyer and politician, Sir John Maynard, who wrote many powerful tracts in their defence, including *The Picklock of the Old Fen Project*. Although no Leveller, Sir John was a critic of Cromwell's growing power, spending the early months of 1648 in the Tower of London (where he met Lilburne) and thereafter condemning the drainage and enclosure of the Fens on the basis of law, custom, liberty and good governance.[11]

In January 1650, Cornelius Vermuyden was appointed director of works for the Great Level drainage, and during the following year, despite what was described in the state papers as the resistance of 'the meaner sort', completed the New Bedford or Hundred Foot River, parallel to what now became the 'Old' Bedford River, which had been dug out fourteen years before.[12] These two massive channels ran straight to the Wash via a giant sluice at Denver, enclosing a flood land which still fills up every winter as its creator intended.

Most of the work to complete these canals was not done by local men. One effective form of resistance remaining to the Fennish was to refuse to provide the labour to dig the drainage channels. Around 11,000 men were employed to cut the New Bedford River, meaning the boycott was a considerable hurdle for the Undertakers to overcome.[13]

One solution was to employ the Scottish prisoners of war taken after the Battle of Dunbar of September 1650 (in which Cromwell defeated a Scottish army loyal to the future King Charles II). However, many Scots deserted with the support of local people, despite a parliamentary order of 19 November 1651 prescribing death to anyone who facilitated the captives' escape.[14] Once England and Scotland reached a settlement the following year, all the prisoners were allowed to return home anyway.

A replacement labour supply was provided by war with the Netherlands. In 1652 about 500 Dutch prisoners were put to work until peace was restored in 1654, but their digging-drudgery was also lightened by the support of local friends. The Adventurers complained in July 1653 that the captives 'not only refuse to work but are encouraged by the

Country people of Swaffham, Waterbeach, Cottenham and other places who are opposite to this work of draining to run away, hiding them in the Corn'.[15]

In the spring of 1651, direct action by the Fennish resumed, with the main focus being on isolated ditches and drains, where the cutting of a single bank could undo a season's work in a matter of hours. In January 1653, cavalry were deployed to protect the works, as horses enabled large areas of drying country to be supervised and retribution raids quickly mounted. After a portion of the Twelve Foot Drain was filled in during the night of 7 February 1653, a squadron of horse from Ely was permanently quartered at Swaffham, near Newmarket.[16]

The presence of soldiers enabled the commissioners to declare in March 1653 that the Great Level had been successfully drained according to the terms of the 1649 Act, meaning that the distribution of enclosed parcels of land could begin. A service of thanksgiving was held in Ely Cathedral on 27 March 1653 – an appropriate venue given that its Chapter and clergy were direct beneficiaries of enclosure.[17] However, the celebration proved to be premature as the following month about 150 Swaffham and Bottisham men rose up and drove all the drainage workers from their common. Cromwell ordered that troops be quartered in the villages until the inhabitants had repaired the damaged works at their own expense. However, the destruction of drains and ditches by 'great numbers of people' continued after dark throughout the summer. From 17 August, a nightly guard of soldiers protected the works in the countryside around Swaffham but it was impossible for them to cover the whole fen. The fact that as a result of the Civil War more of the commoners now had guns, added to the tension.[18]

Two soldiers guarding the Swaffham drainage works were shot and wounded (one seriously, in the head) in August 1653, and two more were forced to throw dirt into a drain as their guards uttered 'very high and insolent speeches'. The identity of the culprits could never be determined, so that all the investigating officer could report was that 'the business is so much in the dark, and so subtly and cunningly carried out … that no Considerable discovery is as yet made neither is there much probability of it for the future'.[19]

Other parts of the great Fen drainage project were also attacked during 1653. In April, works at Methwold Fen in Norfolk were destroyed. The commoners of nearby Stoke Ferry, Dereham and Wretton also took action to protect their wetland, with separate detachments of soldiers being deployed to restore order.[20]

The accounts of the Adventurers reveal that they footed the bill for the military to guard installations, as well as the hefty legal fees required to pursue cases in the courts. The extraordinary sum of £100 was paid to a Huntingdon jury in 1653 to secure a guilty verdict (more than doubling the annual income of most jurors). This was a much larger sum than was usually needed to pay off a jury, indicating that people had to be well rewarded to risk the recriminations that could follow betrayal.[21] Rewards, bonuses and other gratuities were also paid to sheriffs for capturing and prosecuting offenders. Cromwell sought to help Adventurers recover their costs. His 1654 *Ordinance for the Preservation of the Works of the Great Level of the Fenns* 'ordained and established':

> that if any person or persons shall unlawfully cut, cast down, burn or destroy, or other act do for the destroying of any Bank, Dam, Sluce, Salle, Drein or other work made, or to be made, which doth or shall conduce to the Dreining of the said Level, that in such cases the Commissioners ... [shall] award double Dammages to the said Earl, Participants and Adventurers, their heirs and assigns, to be levyed by vitrels and sale of the Offenders goods and for want of sufficient vitrels to commit offenders to the House of Correction, there to remain until satisfaction be made and given of the said damages.[22]

While the deployment of soldiers and courts did have an impact, the critical strategic change was to move from prosecuting individuals to punishing whole communities. Employing the same tactic that would be used to counter the resistance of indigenous people across the empire, 'justice' was now meted out to entire villages.

On the night of 31 January 1654, an enclosure ditch was filled in at Soham Fen. As usual, no offender could be identified but the sheriff decided that 'distresses' should be levied upon the villages nearest to the enclosure to pay for its restoration. In March and April 1654, a bridge was burnt down and drains filled in. Again, adjoining villages were levied to fund the cost of repairs.[23]

The Lord Protector also conferred full citizenship rights on foreign tenants of the enclosed lands. Cromwell's *Ordinance for the Preservation of the Works of the Great Level* ordained 'that if any person or persons of a foreign Nation, in League and Amity with the Common-wealth, being Protestants, shall become purchaser or farmer of any Lands part of the said ninety five thousand acres, the said person or persons, their heirs, executors and Administrators … shall be accounted free Denizons of this Common-wealth'.[24]

The cost of suppressing resistance was further offset by sharing the spoils of victory. A major reorganisation of governance of the Great Level at a meeting of Adventurers in Ely in September 1656 saw the military become a partner with the state in the drainage project. Major General Whalley and Major General Goffe each received 500 acres of drained land, while Cromwell was given a further 200 acres.[25]

There was only sporadic resistance in the Great Level after this. Cromwell's increasingly authoritarian Republic achieved what the divided monarchy had not. Crucial to Commonwealth success was that the new government had the means to enforce its orders. The militias deployed in the 1630s and 40s had comprised local men, many of whom opposed enclosures or were unwilling to take up arms against their neighbours who did, but the battle-hardened Parliamentary warriors were a less conflicted and far more capable force.

Despite the victory on the ground, the propaganda war continued. One pro-commoner pamphlet proclaimed that in the 'late Act for Draining ... injustice, oppression, violence ... are established by a law which ... proceeded from the barren womb of self-interest'; the Undertakers 'destroy not only our pastures and corn ground, but also our poor, and utterly disable us to relieve them'. The drainage project was 'the Philosophers Stone, or that accursed thing ... because it hath proved a Grindstone to the faces of thousands of poor people'. A simple epitaph concluded the entreaty: *He that oppresses the Poor, reproaches his Maker. Prov. 14. 31.*[26]

It had proved unfortunate for the Fennish living in the Great Level region that their fight had become so closely intertwined with the battle for political power in England. As Christopher Hill pointed out over four decades ago: 'The Revolution began with Oliver Cromwell leading fenmen in revolt against court drainage schemes; its crucial turning point was the defeat of the Leveller regiments at Burford, which was immediately followed by an act for draining the fens.'[27]

If the Levellers had been triumphant and the power of the great landed families had been broken (as would occur in France the following century), the Great Level wetlands might have been preserved. This region was drained because the victors in the English Civil War were determined to protect the property rights of the landed class, a reality further confirmed after Cromwell died in 1658 (perhaps hastened on his way by malaria). The restoration of the monarchy institutionalised the new enclosures, with the General Drainage

Act of July 1663 establishing a Corporation for the Great Level, initiating a system of governance that survived until the Corporation was dissolved in 1914. The King received 12,000 of the 95,000 acres set aside for the Adventurers in the Act, with heavy penalties prescribed for those who interfered with works.[28]

Nevertheless, protests continued in the post-restoration decades. After the destruction of drainage works in Mildenhall Fen in 1669, three suspected ringleaders were examined before the Corporation's board on 16 June with King Charles II personally present. Commoner protest was extended in July, with armed commoners firing shots to drive off the guards. Documented resistance at Mildenhall Fen continued until 1684.[29]

But these acts of resistance could no longer hope to over-turn the facts on the ground. By the late seventeenth century, the common wetland of the Great Level seemed to have been vanquished for ever. However, as a more detailed consider-ation of the marshland surrounding the largest lowland lake in England will reveal, the Fennish defeat was never as com-prehensive as the victors' narrative suggests.

CHAPTER 7

The Fight for Whittlesey

The largest lowland lake in England was located about four miles south of the town of Whittlesey, just east of Peterborough. Whittlesey Mere, first documented in the *Anglo-Saxon Chronicle* in a description of estates given by King Wulfhere to Peterborough Abbey, was about 3.5 miles long, east to west, and 2.5 miles north to south, with a depth ranging from two to seven feet.[1] The Mere's reedbed encompassed another 200 acres. The lake was connected to nearby Trundle Mere which in turn was linked to Dray Mere. Surrounding the waters was a vast common wetland of over 7,000 acres.

The Earls of Bedford and Portland enclosed much of this area during the 1630s as part of the Great Level project. Initial resistance was focused on the courts, with repeated suits through the 1630s unsuccessfully challenging the enclosures in the name of customary access that had been 'time out of minde enjoyed'.[2] A petition was presented to the House of

Lords in July 1641 from 'poore Inhabitants of the Towne of Wittlesea' who said enclosure had deprived them of 'their chiefest means of livelihood' and had 'very much impoverished' them.[3]

Ignored by courts and Parliament, in 1643 the commoners resorted to violence to protect their marsh. On 15 May, summoned by the tolling of bells (traditionally used in the Fens as a warning of an approaching flood), two 'companies', each comprising about a hundred inhabitants of Whittlesey and 'loose and disorderly persons' from Ramsey and other nearby villages, were seen wreaking destruction within the enclosures. Armed with spades, forks, shovels, pitchforks and staves, the Fennish dug up coleseed and corn, and broke down the dykes that not only drained the ground but formed the boundary of some of the newly enclosed plots. Hayricks were broken up and their contents used to block the drains.[4] Hundreds of cattle were also turned into crops to 'destroy the same with theire feete' – the herds being driven into land that had previously been open for common grazing.[5]

A 'tumultuous assembly' rampaged through the enclosures around Whittlesey, causing extensive damage to the drained lands. When the local justice, landowner, parliamentarian and Cromwell supporter George Glapthorne ordered the people to disperse, an eyewitness reported that 'Jeffery Boyce, James Boyce, and William Mash held pitchforks against the said George Glapthorne and told him that hee was noe Justice, for hee was against the King, and was all for the Parliament and that they would not obey him nor any Law'.[6]

On 16 May, about 150 Whittlesey and Ramsey commoners began to target farm buildings and threaten tenants. Two
of the new houses erected within the enclosures were pulled
down, one owned by Glapthorne and the other by an equally
prominent Adventurer, Francis Underwood. The attack on a
third house took a more xenophobic form. William Haynes
was seen setting fire to wood and hassocks stacked beside the
home of Peter Behague – one of Whittlesey's 140 colonising
'Walloons' who had crossed from the Low Countries in search
of religious freedom and economic opportunity.[7] Another of
these settlers, James La Roue, was warned that if he continued
to farm he would not 'have his croppe againe'. Two others
were reportedly told that if they ploughed the common, not
only their horses' legs, but also their own would be cut off, for
'it was Commons heretofore and they would have it so still or
else they would lose their lives'.[8]

The local authorities initially seemed powerless to counter
the resistance. Glapthorne did not call on the militia, presumably because one of the three constables, John Boyce, was the
father of several men later identified as resistance leaders, and
would have been equally unlikely to use force against fellow
commoners. Because the rioters were 'not suppresible by the
ordinary Course of Justice', Glapthorne travelled fourteen
miles to Wisbech to seek the assistance of Sir John Palgrave,
the local Parliamentary army commander.[9]

On 17 May about 400 to 500 people were gathered in
Whittlesey ready to resume the reclamation of their common
when around 100 soldiers stopped them entering the enclosed

fen. The soldiers were billeted in the town, at local expense, for about a month.[10] Behague observed that 'had they not gott the sayd number of a hundred souldiers, the sayd ryottours would not have departed thence without making much spoyle'.[11]

As Heather Falvey, the historian who has most closely studied the Whittlesey conflict, has observed, it's unlikely that state authority could have been imposed if Parliamentary troops had not happened to be close by and Glapthorne not sufficiently well connected to the Parliamentary cause to call on them for support. Thirteen people were eventually arrested and brought before the Lords on 10 June. Sixteen days later all were found guilty of an 'outrageous Ryott' and of 'contemptious disobeyinge of the orders of this House' and committed to London's Fleet prison.[12]

Who were the Whittlesey resistance leaders? In his study of Fenland protest, Keith Lindley concluded that they were mostly local gentry whose interests in the common meant they were adversely affected by drainage and enclosure. Clive Holmes questioned Lindley's conclusion on the basis that few substantial gentlemen inhabited Fenland parishes. Falvey's use of local records allowed a more detailed consideration of the commoners' background. She concludes that the original twelve petitioners 'came from a wide cross-section of society … from tenants who were allotted perhaps 130 acres [at enclosure] to men who were landless at that time'.[13] In 1639, some 310 tenants had been allotted nearly 6,000 acres of the enclosed lands but 'ten acres, or even forty, were not considered adequate compensation for their loss' of access to the common.

It must also be remembered that what the common-ers lost when the wetland was drained cannot be measured in economic terms alone. The Fennish were not individ-ual agents focused only on maximising personal wealth as later free-market economic theory assumed everyone to be. Rather, they were a pre-modern people defending their country, culture and community; the relationships that defined their world. The large group of people who received no compensation at all because they had no defined common right suffered the most in material terms from enclosure, but even those who received larger parcels of land were unlikely to see this as compensating for the destruction of their home.[14]

Even the few commoners made relatively wealthy by enclosure were bound by communal and familial connections to people and land. What did they feel when people they had known all their lives were thrown into poverty? When cus-toms and gatherings were discontinued because the resources around which they were based had been lost? When birth sites and sacred places were destroyed? The drainage of the common and the transformation of the landscape destroyed not just a wetland but a way of being. This fact as much as the wealth of the marsh explains why it was not only the poorest folk who resisted the Whittlesey enclosures.

What of the enclosers? What was their background? Falvey's analysis reveals that in 1641 five men were accused of amassing land within the drained fens: George Glapthorne, Francis Underwood, Roger Wiseman, Thomas Boyce and Thomas Ives. Glapthorne, who came from an established Whittlesey family, had fourteen manorial holdings, for which he was allotted 265 acres in the drained fen, the largest allotment granted to any tenant. By 1643 he had purchased more enclosed land, some of it blocking access from the town to the remaining commons. Glapthorne sat on the Commission of Sewers, was a justice of the peace for the Isle of Ely and became a member of Parliament, where he was a strong supporter of the Parliamentary cause. One of Glapthorne's closest associates in promoting drainage and enclosure, Francis Underwood, was a relative newcomer to Whittlesey but was also a parliamentarian. In 1643 Underwood's military service in an action near Peterborough earned him a captain's commission from Cromwell. He eventually rose to the rank of Lieutenant Colonel and in June 1648 was appointed Parliament's 'governor of Whittlesea and Crowland'.[15]

The uneasy peace that accompanied the resistance leaders' release from prison in September 1643 only lasted until the following summer. In July 1644, Nicholas Weston complained to the Lords that his lands had again been entered by 'some ryotous persons' and requested the intervention of 'the Parliament forces thereabouts'. The presence of troops restored a level of calm but on 4 April 1646, commoners 'forcibley' drove animals onto Weston's enclosures and pastured them on the former common land, and the military had to be again actively deployed against the Fennish.[16]

There are few documented acts of resistance after this time, but Falvey points out that the absence of reports in the late 1640s reflects the fact that the House of Lords, to which most petitions and legal actions were presented, had been abolished, and that other sources suggest that the area around Whittlesey was far from peaceful. In June 1648, Colonel Walton, commander of Parliament's troops, reported that he intended to arm 'those that may be trusted. But generally they are disaffected at Wisbish [sic], March, and Whittlesey, whome I purpose to disarme, and to arme honest men if they may be found … I cannot see how that part of the Ile can be secured without a troope of horse upon their frontiers.'[17] Nevertheless, the May 1649 Act for the Draining of the Great Level can be said to mark the end of Fennish independence in this region, as experienced Parliamentary soldiers were deployed to forcefully impose the will of the state.

However, the enclosers' victory was not the end of all resistance. In 1663, the destruction of ditches and fences resumed, with cattle being driven into enclosures. While order was soon restored, there was no permanent peace for the rest of the seventeenth century. As late as January 1699, an estimated 1,100 people attacked drainage works and enclosures just north of Peterborough. These protesters, drawn from a number of surrounding communities, had originally gathered under the 'pretence of Foot ball playing'. During the course of their 'games' they 'did pull upp, Cutt down & destroy the houses buildings, Mills, Banks & Workes of Draining there to the utter Ruin of the said Levell', causing thousands of pounds' worth of damage. The riots threatened to spread. The *Poetic Address to the Marshmen to support the Whittlesey men in the Riots* was a call for Fennish unity: 'In spite of all the Justices Notes', 'Neighbours and friends' were urged to 'meet Whittlesey boys with a Resolution fully Bent'.[18]

The Corporation for the Great Level's response was swift. On 7 March, members of their London office composed a petition, to be presented to King William III the following day, requesting royal orders to secure the Level from 'any Violence or destruction from a rude multitude of desperate & meane people'. On 9 March, the Privy Council wrote letters to the lords lieutenant, high sheriffs and justices of Cambridgeshire, Norfolk, Huntingdonshire and Northamptonshire, and the bailiff of the Isle of Ely, instructing them to use all means necessary to prevent and suppress any riotous assemblies directed against drainage works in the Bedford Level.[19] The prompt and coordinated action of the different arms of an increasingly unified national state (a response unimaginable in its efficiency and scale a century before) prevented the planned assembly.

However, Whittlesey Mere itself survived the drainage of the surrounding marsh. Indeed, the windmills that soon had to be deployed to help the gravity-reliant drains take water to the sea, proved unable to keep many of the new farms permanently dry, let alone drain the lake. Celia Fiennes, who during 1695 rode 'through England on a side saddle', described the celebrated mere:

From Huntingdon we came to Shilton 10 mile and Came in Sight of a great water on the Right hand about a mile off which Looked Like Some Sea it being so high and of great Length; this is in part of the ffenny Country and is Called Whitlsome Mer, is 3 miles broad and six long. In ye Midst is a little island where a great Store of Wildfowle breeds, there is no coming near it; in a Mile or two the ground is all wett and Marshy but there are severall little Channells runs into it which by boats people go up to this place ... There is abundance of good fish in it ...[20]

The mere and its surrounds was a lifeline for dispossessed commoners. While drainage had a dramatic impact on traditional life, the wetlands did not all disappear under the plough. In November 1801, the manor court ordered a committee to record 'the Names of all the Commonable Messuages Cottages and Tolls within the several Manors of Whittlesey', and there proved to be still 364 properties with common rights (just seventeen fewer than had received allotments in 1639).[21] The limits of technology to overcome environmental reality had ensured the survival of significant areas of commons, enabling many Whittlesey commoners to successfully adapt to the latest conquest of their country.

CHAPTER 8

The Battle of Axholme

Since time immemorial, the north Lincolnshire parishes of Epworth, Owston, Haxey, Belton, Althorpe, Luddington and Crowle, and Wroot enjoyed access to a 60,000-acre wetland that sustained, surrounded and protected them. The Domesday Book records that the common marsh of the Isle of Axholme was ten leagues (about 30 miles) long and three leagues wide.[1] The defence of this northern Fenland country became the longest-lasting front in the fight for the Fens. It would also be the site of some of the greatest Fennish victories.

The wealth of the region was based on both daily and seasonal flooding. Much of the marsh was flooded at high tide by the River Trent which formed the eastern boundary of the Isle.[2] In the winter, large areas were replenished with the sediment that fertilised lush pastures in the summer months.

Since the late Middle Ages, the manor that encompassed most of the Isle had been directly held by the monarch. Disinterested royal lordship had benefited the commoners.

Successive princes and kings hunted in the vast 180,000-acre royal forest known as Hatfield Chase but showed little interest in the manor's common wetlands.[3]

However, a year after coming to the throne in 1625, King Charles I did a deal with Cornelius Vermuyden to drain the Isle. The enclosed land was to be divided in thirds between the two men and the commoners. After the King sold his rights to the newly-knighted Vermuyden in 1629, the latter sold on much of his entitlement but continued to direct the project. It soon became evident that the main 'obstruction to this … great undertaking' was, as Abraham De la Pryme observed nearly 300 years ago, 'an old deed of John de Mowbray, once Lord of ye whole island, dated ye 31st of May 1359'.[4]

The commoners had never forgotten the agreement their ancestors had reached with their former lord, Sir John Mowbray.[5] In return for consent to enclosing a portion of land, Mowbray had granted the commoners the remainder of the common free from further restrictions or claims. In effect, the marshland had been handed over to the people of the Isle for their exclusive use. The contract setting this out was kept in the parish church of Haxey in a locked chest bound with iron. More akin to a treaty than a deed, the treasured parchment sat safely in the church for centuries under a stained-glass window depicting Sir John holding it.[6] From the perspective of the commoners, the law was clear: no lord of the manor, be he King or wealthy Dutchman, had a right to encroach on the commons without their consent.

The Axholme Treaty was immortalised in John Hamilton's nineteenth-century novel, *The Manuscript in a Red Box*. The book opens in 1627 with the narrator celebrating the news that the Court of Exchequer had upheld the deed of the Earl of Mowbray, ensuring that the Isle was no longer 'threatened with invasion by one Cornelius Vermuyden, a Dutchman, who had induced the King to grant him authority to drain the meres, embank and stop the rivers of the Isle, and transform the country at his pleasure, regardless of the rights of the Isle Commoners'. The drainage had threatened 'ruin' to 'hundreds of poorer folk, who lived by fishing, fowling, reed-cutting, egg-gathering, and the like crafts of marsh-men'. But the narrated victory is short-lived as the law is debased, politics corrupted and force employed (although softened by the hero falling in love with a Dutch girl, the daughter of one of Vermuyden's command). The book is of particular interest because it depicts the drainers as 'invaders' (a term favoured by commoners but generally shunned by historians) and presents Vermuyden more as an army general than a drainage engineer.

The hostility to drainage and enclosure in the Isle of Axholme did not come only from the late Earl's well-preserved treaty. It was also grounded in an extraordinary equity of access to land. The famous agriculturalist, Arthur Young, observed that:

As to property, I know nothing more singular ... than its great division in the isle of Axholme ... almost every house you see, except very poor cottages on the borders of commons, is inhabited by a farmer, the proprietor of his farm, of from four or five, and even fewer, to twenty, forty, and more acres, scattered about the open fields ... Contrivance, mutual assistance, by barter and hire, enable them to manage these little farms, though they break all the rules of rural proportion.[7]

The prosperity of the small farms came from their access to common pastures and other products from the marsh. The commoners understood that the winter floods brought what they called 'thick fat water' to enrich the common, in contrast to the 'thin, hungry starving water' left after drainage.[8] Flood-driven fertility was the foundation of the flourishing peasant economy which Young had not seen the like of in England.

The wide distribution of land ownership meant that the usual tactic of Adventurers – buying off larger freeholders to claim consent for enclosure – had little chance of success (although it did not stop Vermuyden from trying). The 2,000 or so freeholders of the Isle were a cohesive group who knew their rights and power. Such was their unity that during the summer of 1628, Vermuyden chose to unilaterally commence drainage work without even the pretence of a deal. Not surprisingly, violence soon erupted.[9]

At 2pm on 13 August 1628 in a field south of Haxey, a group of women distracted drainage workers with verbal abuse while the men ambushed them from behind and started throwing volleys of stones. Some of Vermuyden's men were thrown into the dyke and held under with long poles. According to the official report, threats were made to break limbs and burn the men who did not leave the Isle. Improvised gallows were constructed to illustrate the seriousness of their threat, although the intent seems to have been only to frighten the conscripted workers since no one was maimed or killed. Once the work site had been captured, drainage works were destroyed, and wheelbarrows and other implements burned. It was estimated that between 300 and 500 people were involved in the action.

Two days later, Vermuyden moved a well-armed guard into Haxey to teach the people a lesson about the consequences of resistance. Before reaching the village, the invaders were met by a delegation of four unarmed commoners. These men later testified that their offer to negotiate was refused on the basis that the guard's instructions were to 'send them home singing with bullets in their tails'.

When the people did not disperse as instructed, the guard fired indiscriminately into the defenceless crowd. Robert Coggan was shot dead and it seems likely that there was at least one further fatality. A Belton man recounted that another man had died 'standing in defence of his common' and the local clergyman also recalled two burials. Several more commoners were wounded in this indiscriminate attack. Rather than deal with the murders, the Privy Council instructed five local justices to proceed against eighteen commoners and imposed onerous Star Chamber fines that would only be waived on submission to enclosure.[10]

But in defiance of the courts, resistance was renewed at Haxey Carr on 20 September. A group of about 300 commoners, derisively described by Vermuyden as being mainly made up of 'women, boys, servants and poor people whose names cannot be learned', again drove off the workmen and smashed tools and equipment. Work recommenced on 22 September but this led to three days of fighting, in which two workmen were abducted and a boat taken. After the commoners 'scornfully refused' obedience to the orders of a local justice, the Privy Council dispatched a serjeant-at-arms to assist the sheriff and local justices to apprehend 'the principal animators and ringleaders of others'. All were confined pending substantial sureties, and some prosecuted in the dreaded Star Chamber. William Torksey was fined £1,000, an unimaginable sum for a villager. A proclamation from the Attorney General forbidding further hindrance of drainage work was read in the centre of Haxey by the serjeant-at-arms accompanied by the sheriff and other officers defended by 30 cavalry. The order was accompanied by a threat to sack and burn the whole town if there were further disturbances.[11]

Nevertheless, in the summer of 1629 resistance resumed. At the end of July over 350 commoners, mainly women, destroyed one of the new dykes over three days. Two commoners were taken to Lincoln Castle, and nine women prosecuted in the Star Chamber were among fourteen people subject to crushing fines. But the tumult continued until 27 August when the Privy Council ordered the sheriff to raise the power of the county to suppress attacks and imprison offenders. With

Vermuyden empowered to use the militia, the fight for the Isle was being treated as a war, the drainage work proceeding under military protection. Not surprisingly, the presence of well-armed soldiers temporarily restored a degree of order.[12]

The 'peace' allowed drainage works to be sufficiently completed to bring in settlers to colonise the drained land. The new village of Sandtoft, complete with a French Protestant church, was built to accommodate them.[13] Archbishop Neile of York estimated that about 200 foreign families moved into the Isle to 'take the bread out of the mouths of English subjects'. The Archbishop was not an objective observer – he was opposed to this rival Protestant church being established in England – but the fact that the congregation at Sandtoft in 1645 numbered over 1,000 means that, in regard to numbers, Neile was not exaggerating the impact of colonisation.[14]

Once placed in their new homes, the settlers became highly vulnerable to attack. On 12 July 1633 it was reported that commoners had 'trod the writs under their feet' and threatened 'to kill the servants of the Dutch, rip up their bellies and throw their hearts in their faces'. The military was called in to restore order and more Fennish were imprisoned.

The next year, attacks were largely confined to the night so that it became more difficult to identify participants in the resistance. The drainers claimed that in May alone, under cover of darkness, over £2,000 damage was done to property. Vermuyden's response was to seek collective punishment, with financial pressure brought to bear on the whole community at the very time that access to food and income was being reduced by the drainage works. In October, a court case was deliberately held in distant Lincoln, where a carefully chosen jury of unsympathetic townsmen ordered damages of £2,500 to be paid by the Isle villages.

Vermuyden sought to further divide the commoners by offering to waive the share of the fine owed by any individual who signed the enclosure agreement. About 370 commoners, otherwise facing financial ruin and homelessness, were reported to have done this. But even this number was nowhere near the necessary majority.[15] Under extraordinary pressure, the community was holding firm.

A further inducement to consent to enclosure was contained in concessions granted by the Attorney General, Sir John Banks, on 7 June 1636. While this order confirmed the earlier division of land, it allowed commoners the liberty to crave royal pardon to relieve all individual and collective fines (with the implication that this would be granted if consent was given to enclosure), and the allocation of £400 by participants to provide stock to employ the poor.[16]

Legal action continued against individuals, although local justices, juries and constables could still provide protection. Belton had a succession of constables who refused to execute warrants. One even actively helped the commoners by arranging for guards to prevent the impounding of their cattle.[17]

The conflict continued up to the Civil War and beyond. It was a multi-faceted campaign involving appeals to King, Parliament, aristocrats, custom and law; as well as diverse direct actions. Cattle were effectively employed in the fight through being driven into tenants' crops; peat and hay were cut in enclosures to assert customary rights; and commoners continually entered 'private property' to try to secure a trial that would test the legitimacy of the Mowbray deed. Vermuyden tacitly acknowledged his legal vulnerability by not succumbing to the provocation to prosecute anyone for trespass.

As in southern Fenland, the breakdown of centralised authority during the Civil War benefited the resistance. In June 1642 (according to a later appeal for compensation from Parliament), 'some of the Inhabitants thereabout … taking advantage of the distractions of those times, rose in tumults, break down the fences and inclosures of 4,000 acres, destroyed all the Corn growing, and pulled down the Houses built thereon'. In February 1646, Parliament sent '100 persons to restore order' but they were confronted by 400 men, who 'forced the Sheriff with all his assistants to flie, and then demolished what the Sheriff had before caused to be set up'. Inhabitants then 'laid waste the remaining 3,400 acres' of colonised country.

A Lords order of 10 December 1646 for the suppression of riots within the manor of Epworth was dismissed by commoners with the retort that 'they did not care a Fart for the Order which was made by the Lords in Parliament and published in the Churches, and that notwithstanding that Order, they would pull down all the rest of the Houses in the Level that were built upon these Improvements which were drained and destroy all the Enclosures'.[18]

On 20 May 1647, about 43 men and women attacked workmen with pitchforks, clubs and stones, seriously wounding two of them, as they tried to erect fences and clear drains. On 22 May, more drains were destroyed, and when the sheriff tried to intervene, one of his men was wounded in the head by a sword.[19]

The resistance in Axholme initially benefited from the commoners' identification with the Parliamentary cause. The key figure here was Daniel Noddel (1611–72), who held the rank of Lieutenant in the Parliamentary forces. Noddel acted as the commoners' attorney and solicitor from about 1646 to 1662 as well as leading local reprisals and actions. However, the support provided by prominent Levellers proved problematic once Cromwell's victory had been achieved.

The parliamentary committee that conducted an inquiry into the conflict during 1650 noted that Noddel had obtained the 'assistance of Lieut Colonel John Lilburn and Major John Wildman'. They found that in the previous year the commoners, under the influence of these men, 'declared they would not give any Obedience thereunto, nor to any order of the Exchequer or Parliament'; 'some said it was a Parliament of clouts, and that if they sent any Forces, they would raise Forces to resist them'. A total of 82 'Habitations' were destroyed, 'besides Barns, Stables and other Outhouses', as well 'all Corn and rapes' on 3,400 acres of land.

The inquiry documented with alarm that Lilburne had led the commoners to Sandtoft church on a Sunday 'where the French Congregation of Protestants were gathered and forced them from thence'. The crowd then marched on to Crowle, where the tenants 'being thus terrified, and seeing their condition was to be like their neighbours', also fled.

Lilburne took up temporary residence in the riot-damaged home of the minister of Sandtoft (with his cows comfortably sheltered in the empty chapel), from where he acted as negotiator, legal adviser and propagandist for the cause. This commitment was not entirely selfless. In October 1651, Lilburne, Wildman and Noddel reached an agreement with the commoners to continue to represent them in return for receiving land.[20]

In May 1651, an Exchequer decree sanctioned further action to restore order in the Isle, but the commoners promised 'a bloody day' if soldiers were used to enforce what they described as 'orders not worth 2d'. When the decree was read out to them, it was reported that one Belton man exclaimed 'they would neither obey the Barons nor Parliament ... it was a traitorous Order', while the well-named William Wash was reported to have added that 'they could make as good a Parliament themselves'. To prove their point, in June 1651 over 80 houses, outbuildings, a windmill and surviving crops belonging to colonists were destroyed. This well-organised action by men and women working in groups of 20 to 100 or more saw Sandtoft in ruins and all of the old commons secured.[21]

Historian Keith Lindley suggests that the hostility to parliamentary orders in May and June was counter to the advice of Noddel, Lilburne and Wildman, who put greater faith in the legal process. He argues that increasingly independent actions by local resistance leaders acts as a caveat 'against the temptation to view rioters through the eyes of the authorities who almost invariably regarded them as manipulated from above'.[22]

In 1652, Lilburne was fined, banished from Parliament, and exiled for two years – a 1651 tract, *The Case of the Tenants of the Manor of Epworth in the Isle of Axholme in the County of Lincoln* being his enduring testament to the commoners' cause. Lilburne never returned to the Isle although Wildman continued to act as legal counsel in London.[23]

Parliament was dissolved before the committee looking into the conflict could present its report, but it was considered by the Council of State. On 12 July 1653 the Council, concerned about the 'insurrections', 'public peace' and 'danger of the commonwealth', ordered that neighbouring armed forces be made available to the sheriff to maintain order. The 'Forces of the Army quartering in the said Levell of Hatfield Chase or within the Said Counties of Yorke, Lincolnshire and Nottingham' were ordered to restore enclosed land to the new landlords, ensure reparation was paid to them, prevent protests and punish protesters. The wider context of this assertion of state power was a concern to put the Levellers in their place (this being, in some cases, the Tower or scaffold).

The fate of the commoners rested directly with the Lord Protector after a report from the Commission of Sewers in January 1655 starkly presented the resistance as a rebellion against Cromwell himself. The commissioners claimed that in October 1654, inhabitants 'being armed as aforesaid, came in a riotous manner, and being charged by the Sheriff in Your Highness Name, to lay down their Arms and repair to their several dwellings', they 'not only refused to give obedience but some of them with scandalous and opprobrious language of the person of Your Highness, and with diverse affronts and menaces, caused the Sheriff and his company to depart away for fear of their lives'. Furthermore, several persons and officers had declared 'that they dare not go in the Isle … upon execution of certain Orders of them directed, without manifest danger of their lives'.

That the one-time 'Lord of the Fens' still harboured some residual sympathy for the commoners' cause is suggested by the fact that when he handed the problem over to General Edward Whalley it was not to forcefully restore order but to inquire further into what was going on. Sympathy for the refugee tenant farmers was also apparent in the instructions to inquire into 'the business of the poor Protestant Strangers'. The General's report, delivered in June 1656, confirmed the level of destruction and violence, including the desecration of the church.[24] In August, Cromwell ordered Whalley to restore order, prevent riots, return estates, and ensure the free exercise of religion. He was also not to allow the inhabitants of the Isle 'to keep by them Armes or other Instruments for the further acting of such disorders'. From now on, the army was to directly assist the sheriffs and Court of Sewers to implement government orders.[25]

On the ground, though, little rebuilding work was undertaken. The security situation seems to have still been considered too risky for colonisers to return to their farms or for investors to spend the money on drainage works and the rebuilding of Sandtoft. In December 1660, the Lords ordered that all enclosed land be restored to its owners. Robert Reading, who had bought up most of the Adventurers' claims, levied a tax on commoners for what he claimed was owed in damages. Over 50 villagers then attacked Reading and his men, dragging them from their horses and wounding several. Reading alleged that when he told the people that he was there in the newly restored King's name to execute the orders of the House of Lords, he was told 'that they would obey neither King, nor Lords, nor Laws'. Violent fighting continued into the evening in Hatfield, with documented fatalities on both sides. One of Reading's men, John Patterwick, was killed by blows to the head; while William Lockier was shot through the right thigh, allegedly by Reading himself, dying a week later.[26]

Conflict continued throughout 1661, with many commoners prosecuted and imprisoned. Thomas Vavasour, one of the wealthier resistance leaders and freeholder of Epworth (whose name had been used in legal suits because he was a direct descendant of one of the commoners named in the original agreement with the Earl of Mowbray), was gaoled in London in 1662 and lost almost all his property. Daniel Noddel acted for commoners for the last time in May 1662, dying the following decade with total wealth of less than £50.[27]

The endless court cases and ongoing sabotage were costly for both sides. It was the sheer persistence and unity of the commoners and their capacity to destroy expensive infrastructure that made them so difficult to defeat. It was impossible to maintain a constant military guard over the vast fen or identify all those involved in destroying property and drains when the whole community was implicated. Worn down by years of fighting, in 1666 Reading temporarily gave up his lands to the commoners, with the exception of the two acres at Sandtoft where his own house stood.[28]

There were some attempts at arbitration over the ensu-ing decades but it was not until 1691 that an agreement was reached under which most of the formerly-enclosed fen-land was divvied out in plots that were mostly allocated to commoners. Many of the local people still saw this deal as a betrayal and renewed resistance, led by Catherine and Robert Popplewell of Belton, saw fences ripped up, crops destroyed, Reading and his sons shot at, their cattle slaughtered and their house pulled to the ground. Catherine was indicted in 1694 but escaped with a small penalty in return for her husband promising to work for peace. However, attacks continued under the cover of darkness.[29] Around midnight on 15 April 1697, Reading's new home was destroyed by fire. Later that year, his outbuildings, orchards, gardens and farming imple-ments were plundered by commoners, who returned to Belton to dine on their foe's pigs and poultry. Some ringleaders were subsequently declared outlaws and had to flee the county, although Robert Popplewell disassociated himself from the protests after he was ordered to pay Reading £600.[30]

The result of the uncompromising resistance was that at the end of the seventeenth century, the majority of supposedly enclosed country was still being managed as a common marsh. The culture this created was exposed by the arrival of a new vicar of Epworth, Samuel Wesley. In a 1701 letter appealing for funds to The Society for Promoting Christian Knowledge, Wesley described his new parish in some detail. There was no school for the 7,000 people and less than one in twenty of the population could recite the Lord's Prayer. There were no Roman Catholics or Presbyterians in the parish but there were about 40 Quakers and 70 Anabaptists who insulted the vicar wherever he went (both radical Christian groups were long established in the Isle). Wesley had instigated a monthly service of Holy Communion but no more than twenty attended and hardly anyone in the parish would assist him.[31]

In 1702, the Epworth rectory was burnt and about three-quarters of the building lost, before it was totally destroyed by a second fire in 1709. All the Wesley family were evacuated except for the small boy who would become the founder of Methodism. John Wesley had to be pulled from a second-floor window as the building was engulfed in flames. Susanna Wesley thereafter believed that her son was a 'brand plucked from the burning' and this Bible verse formed the epitaph of John Wesley's best-selling journal. It was also the inscription under Henry Parker's picture of Epworth rectory in flames which found a place in many nineteenth-century Methodist homes, school rooms and vestries.[32] Writing a century after the event, W.B. Stonehouse pointed to a continuing oral tradition that the fire was arson, observing that 'there is some reason to think that both these conflagrations were the work of an incendiary'.[33] Given that Samuel Wesley was a conservative Church of England minister whose sympathies would clearly have been with the enclosing landlords, this seems a believable claim.

The last serious conflict in the Isle occurred between 1712 and 1714. Reading's remarkable endurance probably helped the cause of peace; somehow, he survived to be over 100, by which time his sons had been effectively assimilated into Fennish life. While it is hard to verify, it seems that some form of understanding was reached which meant that, so long as tenants stayed in their allocated lands, and there was no further attempt to encroach on the common or disrupt customary rights, they would be left in peace. This uneasy status quo remained in place for a century.

Most of the Isle of Axholme was not enclosed until 1795. Even then, part of the common marsh and many of the open fields were protected. Arthur Young, writing in the late eighteenth century, observed that there were still 66,000 acres of fens 'not begun to be drained' (although some of this wetland would be lost by 1808). Young thought it was also 'a most barbarous omission, that when this [1795 Enclosure] act was procured, they [the commoners] resisted a clause to divide the open arable fields, subject to rights of common'.[34]

An attempt to enclose these fields in 1803 was defeated. An 1813 Act did enclose most of Crowle, Eastoft and Ealand but even then some open fields remained. Writing in the 1830s, W.B. Stonehouse blamed the lack of a continuing lord of the manor for 'the great error of leaving the fields open in

Epworth, Haxey, Owston and Belton', as well as the failure to progress 'spending improvements ... by which the low grounds on the west side would have been effectively drained, and 20,000 acres of land improved'.[35]

Stonehouse also observed that a remarkably equitable distribution of land and wealth still characterised the Isle: 'The lands in the Isle of Axholme are divided among a greater number of owners than in any other part of the kingdom. There are many small freeholders, holding from twenty acres of land to one single rood.'[36] This equity had endured precisely because enclosure had been successfully resisted. Far from being a futile attempt to hold back the inevitable march of modernity, the actions of the Axholme Fennish had allowed them to prosper by successfully resisting the drainage of their wetland home.

CHAPTER 9

Victory in Lincolnshire

The wetlands surrounding Boston in southern Lincolnshire were the final front in the fight for the Fens. The plan to enclose this country was contemporaneous with the drainage plans for the Great Level and the Isle of Axholme and, like the latter, was a scheme hatched in the Royal Court. From 1631, Sir William Killigrew and other well-placed courtiers around the King began to plot how the marsh could be drained to the benefit of themselves and the Crown.

These wetlands were particularly large and productive. The common of just one of them, Holland Fen, covered 22,000 acres north-west of Boston and supported eleven villages with a combined population of over 4,000. Frampton had about 500 residents despite only having about 125 acres of arable land. Horses, sheep, cattle and geese grazed in the summer pastures, with value added through the dairy, hides, tallow, feathers, and spinning cottage industries. The familiar fish, wildfowl, reeds and hay were also directly harvested from the fen.[1]

Resistance to the enclosure of Holland Fen was antici-
pated and the strategy to overcome it was set out in a 1635
document written by one of the King's advisers. A commission was to be established to inquire into 'certain particulars'
whose adverse findings and tax impositions would 'much
conduce the commoners to desire a composition [settle-
ment]'. The next step would be 'a legal prosecution of some
principal opposers', after which 'the country being thus
perplexed, and their leaders taken off, and all the fen taxed ...
certain gentlemen ... Will make [the commoners] sensible of
their case ... and if they be then willing to give such a proportion as his Majesty shall think fit to accept (which I conceive
will be at least 10,000 acres) a commission may be issued to
fit persons to treat and compound [enclose]'.[2]

The commission that conducted the inquiry included the
Earl of Lindsey and Sir William Killigrew, the men who had
planned the operation from the start. Unsurprisingly it found
that the fen was 'surrounded by water', and imposed a tax
to fund the engineering works to change this. In June 1637,
they contracted with the King to drain Holland Fen; he then
subcontracted the Earl of Lindsey and other Undertakers to
do this work in return for a share in the land.[3]

The commoners petitioned Parliament in protest, pointing
out that the rich summer pastures were sustained by annual
flooding and listing the abundance of 'reeds, fodder, thacks,
turves, flags, hassocks, segg, fleggweed for fleggeren, collors,
mattweede for churches, chambers, beddes and many other

fenn commodytyes of greate use both in towne and countreye' that came directly from the wetland.[4]

The King's close association with the drainage schemes meant that the Privy Council, Star Chamber, Duchy Court and Court of Exchequer dismissed all legal claims against enclosure and facilitated the prosecution of protesters. But the commoners refused to submit according to plan, and armed resistance soon broke out. Sir Anthony Thomas complained of the great damage done to his lands 'by the assemblies of divers [diverse] riotous and unruly persons', and by 1636 the Privy Council was receiving numerous other reports of 'divers insolencies' by inhabitants of East and West Keale, High and Low Toynton and adjacent towns.

Between 6 and 8 August 1636, an estimated 400 to 500 people marched to the sound of a drum under the command of two men 'who termed themselves the Captain and the Lieutenant', and began to fill in ditches. After this brigade were warned that force would be brought in against them, they reportedly replied that 'they feared no suppressing, for the next day they could have 500 come to them, and the next day after, more'.

It was only after the 'Captain' and 'Lieutenant' leading the uprising – the Freiston labourer Edmond Clipsham, and William Richardson (whose 'abode and station' were not known) – were incarcerated at Lincoln gaol, and under interrogation revealed the names of others actively engaged in the resistance, that the state restored a semblance of order.

Killigrew also took independent action, admitting that after 'some poor men' had cut drains and driven cattle into the Undertaker's corn, he seized the commoners' cattle, returning them only 'upon their submission [to enclosure] and tears'. Not all the locals were so easily won over: Thomas Kirke was offered 'the like favour … which he rejected and by persevering in his riots did compel the drainers to distrain his cattle and sell them'.[5]

The power of the Crown meant that the fens between the River Witham and the coast were successfully drained and enclosed during the mid-1630s. However, by decade's end, fighting had resumed.

In 1640, the Earl of Lindsey petitioned Parliament to take stronger action against persons who 'have not only excited the meaner sort of people, but have themselves likewise in a tumultuous and illegal manner entered upon divers parts of the lands allotted … thrusting their cattle into the same and keeping them there with force and violence, and have likewise cut the banks and works in several places, and will not permit petitioner's agents and workmen to repair the same'.[6] But during the winter of 1640–41, commoners assembled 'in great troops' to level enclosures. A further desperate appeal was made to Parliament on the grounds that the riots could 'beget a rebellion'.[7]

Resistance further intensified in the summer of 1641. On 30 June, two men and fifteen women from Donington herded cattle into enclosures in Helpringham Fen that belonged to Lindsey and Killigrew. On 8 July, the Earl again appealed to the Lords for emergency action, pointing out that commoners had 'assembled themselves together in Companies and troops consisting of many hundreds' to demolish banks and destroy crops, and were now threatening to pull down or burn houses belonging to Undertakers and their tenants.[8]

The new landlords then petitioned the Commons on 10 July for protection, but received little support. This emboldened the Fennish, and a troop of Donington men and women launched a well-organised invasion of enclosed land on 12 August. Rather than destroying the crops, they carted them away after they had overseen their harvest by the Undertakers' tenants. About 40 cartloads of corn, rye and hemp were taken over four to five days, with any farmers who refused to cooperate being beaten.[9]

Not only did the local justice, William Lockton, refuse to hear claims against the commoners but he committed one 'Dutch' settler to Lincoln gaol for eight days for assaulting a woman who was taking his crop of rye. A number of other tenants were also arrested. Lockton was said to have remarked that 'by God's blood he cared not a fart for the best Undertaker in England', and further swore: 'By God's blood neighbours you shall not be wronged.'[10]

On 2 August, a crowd from Sibsey filled in ditches and drove cattle into the enclosure. On 7 August they extended their action, proceeding 'with a fiddler playing before them'. The protests that continued for a couple of weeks included the burning down of houses, seizure of the flax harvest and destruction of crops.

Some arrests were made at the end of August but these only served to further enrage the commoners. Fennish leaders openly proclaimed themselves willing to die for their cause and by early September, Parliament was being warned that a general rebellion was imminent. The sheriff, Sir Edward Heron, unsuccessfully sought to enforce the orders of the Lords through deploying armed militia. Attempts to restore enclosed lands in Horbling, Billingborough and Quadring through the courts were equally futile, as juries repeatedly sided with the commoners.[11]

During April 1642, large crowds assembled at the houses in Boston where Fennish prisoners were being held. One thousand people were reported to have freed Thomas Pishey and Richard Sibsey. The crowd then pursued Heron and other justices, shouting abuse and pelting them with stones and dirt until they reached the town limits. The Mayor of Boston subsequently refused to execute a warrant to arrest the offenders.[12]

The Undertakers reported to the Lords that 'many hundreds' of commoners had destroyed works costing nearly £60,000, demolished several houses and assaulted the sheriff and justices. What was described as 'a general confederacy' had even set up its own legal system. Commoners had 'at several places and sessions indicted the said Sheriff and Justices and some of their servants', and juries were refusing to punish the rebels. The Undertakers believed that a final assault was being planned for 13 May in which all the surviving works and houses in enclosed country would be destroyed. In response to this plea, the Lords authorised the raising of the power of the county and required local officers and clergy to read out an order outlining the consequences of resistance in all villages and churches. However, 'many hundreds' ignored these warnings and marched into the fen 'in troop after Captains' where they pulled down eleven houses, destroyed works, levelled enclosures, moved in cattle and fired crops. Anyone who tried to stop them was assaulted.

Killigrew's own newly-built house was attacked on 16–17 May but successfully defended. The commoners then increased their number by recruiting in Spalding on market day. Thus strengthened, about 500–600 people assembled near the well-fortified building on 19 May. A cannon shot was fired into the crowd but they still refused to disperse, reportedly warning the defenders that 'if any of their company were killed or hurt, they would not leave a man or woman alive that was in the house', and that even if they failed 'there was a thousand more would second them'. The attack began about 6pm, and over a four- to five-hour period the property and its contents were totally destroyed. Those of Killigrew's servants who did not cooperate were ducked in one of the new drains. Killigrew himself was fortunate not to be present when the raid occurred.

Victory was secured throughout the southern Lincolnshire fenlands in the spring of 1642. The Fennish pulled down about a further 50 houses and barns, with some occupants reportedly dragged out by their heels. Witnesses who gave evidence against commoners in lawsuits were targeted, as were men who worked for the justices and sheriffs. The leaders were again reported to have declared 'they would lose their lives before they would desist' in their resistance.[13]

The close association between the drainers and the Crown (Killigrew would command one of the two troops of horse that guarded the King during the conflict) ensured that the comprehensive Fennish victory was sustained after the Civil War. A London-centred campaign that relied on the power of the monarch and the institutions he controlled was destined for defeat once royal authority was lost. The commoners were quick to point out to Parliament that Lindsey and Killigrew fought for the King but 'We ... fought with the Parliament, For Law, Liberty and our Rights, against oppression'. Another reason that neither Parliament nor Cromwell sought to moderate or overturn the Fennish victory in the way they did elsewhere was that these lands had been drained without local gentry involvement – meaning that the legitimacy of old property rights was not at stake.[14]

However, these dynamics do not fully explain the *permanency* of the victory achieved. Despite repeated attempts by the drainers to have the enclosed lands returned after the restoration of the monarchy, the Fennish secured their country not just for a decade but for the next century. Killigrew, Sir Henry Heron (heir of Sir Edward) and fellow Undertakers had statutes prepared in August 1660 and May 1661 which had the support of King Charles and passed the Lords. However, the House of Commons refused to support them, as it did ten further bills between 1666 and 1685. The heirs of the

Adventurers pressed their claim for the enclosed land for decades, with parliamentary recognition sought in 1698, 1700, 1701, 1705 and 1711, but still the enclosures were not restored. Legislative attempts to retrieve lands in Holland and the surrounding fens were equally futile. With the sole exception of Wildmore Fen, whose enclosure was recognised in law, the commoners' victory seemed secure.[15]

With the common safe, the population of the Lincolnshire fenland almost doubled between 1563 and 1723 (whereas in arable parts of the same county, the population stayed roughly the same).[16] When Daniel Defoe visited the southern Lincolnshire fens in the early eighteenth century, he raved about their wealth and beauty:

> The country around this place [Boston] is all fen and marsh grounds, the land very rich, and which feeds prodigious numbers of large sheep, and also oxen of the largest size, the ... best of which goes to the London market; and from this part ... comes the greatest part of the wool, known, as a distinction for its credit, because of its fineness, by the name of Lincolnshire wool; which is sent in great quantities into Norfolk and Suffolk, for the manufacturers of those counties ... Here are also an infinite number of wildfowl, such as duck and mallard, teal and widgeon, brand geese, wild geese, &c.[17]

There was little change in the decades after Defoe's visit. *Bingley's London Journal* of 31 October 1772 suggests that there were 'at least six thousand useful poor inhabitants' still enjoying the use of Holland Fen.[18]

What explains the longevity of the Fennish victory? Investors long remained nervous of the large losses suffered by the Earl of Lindsey, which were thoroughly documented by the Adventurers themselves. An unintended impact of the tracts written by Killigrew and the equally eloquent William Dugdale was to discourage anyone else from taking the commoners on. But the key reason for the long-term survival of the wetland was the range of people who shared in the wealth they produced.

The distribution of common wealth reflected the fact that this region, like the Isle of Axholme, had no aristocracy – here was no Earl of Bedford to push the enclosure through: 'The want of gentlemen here to inhabit' was a fact lamented by officials in Holland in the muster returns as early as 1580.[19] In the late eighteenth century, Arthur Young contrasted the situation in nearby Revesby, where Sir Joseph Banks was a large landowner and activist encloser, drainer and 'improver', with that of the Fennish district of South Holland where 'property is very much divided, and freeholds numerous'. Young documented that in the parish of Freiston, containing about 3,000 acres, there is 'not one plot of more than 48 acres together belonging to one person'.[20]

The wide distribution of wetland wealth extended to Boston itself, where many merchants and leading citizens had rights in the common or profited from its products. Killigrew complained bitterly in 1653 about 'those that have and are now pullinge that greate slues [sluice] to peeces at Boston Towne's Ende, which cost about sixe thousand pounds'.[21] He warned that 'the sea will breake in all that side of the country' but the dire warnings of flooding, which carried such propaganda power in London, had little impact locally where the people relied on floodwaters for their prosperity. Because it was known that the engineering schemes were designed to drain the land, not protect it, the townsmen who set fire to the 'Great Sluice' ensured that it remained in disrepair for a century. The movement of water had been managed for centuries, with the vast marshland catchments limiting the flooding of towns and villages. The people of the Fens knew that they lived with the possibility of a catastrophe but believed that the dangers posed by rapidly rising waters were only amplified in drained country. For the Fennish, the wetland was perceived not as a problem to be overcome but as the foundation of their freedom.

CHAPTER 10

The Foundation of Fennish Freedom

In 1700 it seemed that the culture and community life based around the common marsh had been permanently protected outside the Great Level. The successful resistance of the Fennish was based on their capacity to meet basic needs without succumbing to state, employer or landlord power. Their ability to obtain food, clothing, shelter and income directly from the natural environment meant that the people of the Fens did not have to submit in order to survive.

Historians disagree on how much difference the resources of the common made to ordinary English people by the eighteenth century. The evidence suggests that large numbers of commoners were dependent on wages long before formal enclosure took place (which could be a piecemeal process over generations). However, this debate does not extend to the Fens, where there is no dispute concerning the significance of the common or the level of disruption associated with drainage and enclosure.[1] In Donington near Boston in 1767, it was recorded that 100 per cent of labourers were keeping cows; at Shouldham in Norfolk, 56 per cent of labourers owned cattle as late as 1794. Access to a single cow could provide a return of five to six shillings per week in the late eighteenth century, roughly equivalent to an agricultural labourer's wage.[2]

The agriculturalist Arthur Young recognised that the commons of Lincolnshire ensured that 'land, gardens, cows, and pigs, are so general in the hands of the poor', meaning that 'poor-rates are low; upon an average of the county, they do not amount to one third of what is paid in Suffolk'.[3]

The freedom conferred by the common remained particularly important for women (whose right to 'reasonable estovers★ of commons' was even acknowledged in the Magna Carta). The cow-owning widow of 'Jack and the Beanstalk', dependent on common pastures for her livelihood, was based on historical reality (as were the stories of dispossessed village women surviving in large towns in any way they could).[4]

The economic independence of the Fennish was a serious problem for landowners, tenant farmers and drainage engineers seeking not only submission to their enclosure plans but a subservient labour force. The commons were rightly recognised to promote 'indiscipline and indolence among the workers' because they meant that people's survival did not depend on them accepting the discipline of waged work.[5] The reason that immigrants had to be employed on engineering schemes and enclosed farms was primarily because

★ A right to collect wood from the commons.

the locals had an attractive alternative available to them.[6] This competition also meant that higher wages had to be paid. Young observed that labour costs in the Lincolnshire fens were 'probably higher than in any other county in the kingdom'.[7]

The freedom of the commons was grounded in not just the quantity but the range of resources available. James C. Scott has described wetlands as places of 'fugitive diversity' because the variety of birds, fish, and animals returning at predictable times allowed ordinary people to access what they needed without the rigours and risks of conventional farming.[8] Unlike the taxed, tithed and rent-paying tenant farmer, whose harvest could fail, leaving hunger and debt in its wake, the Fennish commoner had a range of alternative food supplies. When the meadows were too wet to graze or cut for hay, fishing and hunting conditions improved. When the marsh receded, the pastures expanded.

Wetland fecundity means that even cow ownership is a less accurate measure of common wealth in the Fens than in more ecologically restricted parts of England. Consider the wealth available from the meat, eggs and feathers of geese alone – which even the poorest Fennish family had access to. The first pluck after Lady Day (6 April) was for feathers and quills, with the four subsequent annual plucks used for feathers alone. Flocks were attended by a gizzard or goose-herd (likely to be one of the children) who twice a day drove them to water. Surplus birds were sold for meat for the increasingly lucrative London market. The domestic geese of the Fennish were probably descended from the greylag which bred wild in the wetland, and these migratory geese were also an important source of meat, feathers and eggs.[9]

Many other wild birds were also accessed for their meat and eggs, including bittern, mallard, snipe, teal, swan, crane, spoonbill and heron (despite Henry VII forbidding the killing of the latter, a favourite sporting bird, except by hawk and longbow). Birds were traditionally driven into nets or caught in traps but the adaptability of Fennish culture is shown by the seventeenth-century adoption of the Dutch technique of decoys.[10] This required constructing ponds that had channels dug off them which domestic ducks swam up to be fed, while the wild birds following them were trapped in nets. Daniel Defoe observed 'that it is incredible what quantities of wild-fowl of all sorts, duck, mallard, teal, widgeon, &c., they take in those duckoys every week, during the season. It may indeed be guessed at a little by this, that there is a duckoy not far from Ely ... that they generally sent up [to London] three thousand a week.'[11]

Until the mid-nineteenth century, guns were ineffective and costly by comparison with alternative hunting methods; although the new punt guns (effectively small cannons fitted onto the boats that could kill up to 25 birds in a single shot) were certainly horribly efficient killing machines.[12]

Fishing also continued to be important to the economic security of the Fennish. Conically-shaped eel traps or 'hives', made from willow, were baited with a piece of rotten flesh such as a dead bird or rodent. Eels could be eaten boiled or cold with little preparation other than gutting, or preserved in oil for leaner times. Their skins provided clothing, hats, string, and even wedding rings.

Eels as well as other fish, including pike, roach and perch, were also caught in fish weirs. The origins of these wooden fish traps, which were placed across the current between an island and the bank (with the other side of the island left open for navigation and for some fish to move between waters), went back to Anglo-Saxon times.[13]

Critical to the freedom of the fen was that the technology needed to hunt and access resources was also freely available from the natural environment. Boats, nets, traps and glaives (pronged spears) were made from willow and other local wood. The punt that would be romanticised by Cambridge University students was a handmade Fennish boat ideal for quiet movement through the marsh.[14]

It was not only food that was freely available from the fen, but also fuel, shelter, and clothing. Peat fires never went out in Fennish houses. So important was peat that one mid-nineteenth-century observer recorded that 'portions of the fen are purposely kept in a partially undrained state, for the sake of the peat, or turf, as it is locally called'. In 1877, the geologist Sydney Skertchly recorded that peat was still the 'favourite fuel of the Isle of Ely' and a century later, elderly people still recalled their families digging 'turf' from the fen when they were children.[15]

Housing was another essential of life that commoners could build, repair and replace for themselves. Arthur Young observed the brick and tile cottages of the new tenant farmers in the early nineteenth century but also documented the traditional timber dwellings, 'walled with clay, called stud and mud'. The hazel or willow studs, as 'large as a man's arm', could be replaced as readily as the walls. Interiors were lined with hides, fleeces, skins or feathers for insulation, while roofs were thatched with reed. Most cottages had no chimney, with smoke escaping just through a hole in the roof, but the peat smoke helped keep out biting midges and mosquitoes. Vernacular houses could be built wherever shelter was needed. Arthur Young met a man called 'Talbot, a poor man of Downham', who 'six years ago built himself a hut in this fen with a few stakes laced with bundles of sedge, and plastered ... for carrying on his labour of cutting sedge, turf, and fishing'. Young noted that Talbot, his wife and four children 'had their health to the full ... though in winter the water surrounded his cottage, so that he could get to and from it only in his boat'.[16]

Fennish housing was designed to last for decades, not centuries, meaning that it has now vanished from the landscape. But its suitability to the local environment is evident from the continuity in design over many centuries. Writing in the 1870s, J.M. Heathcote quotes an earlier description of Fennish architecture: 'small, rustical and wild; the fashion of their houses had changed little since the days of the ancient Britons. The houses or huts were of round shape, and not unlike the forms of beehives. They had a door in front, and an opening at the top to let out the smoke, but window to let in the light there was none.'[17]

The resources of the marsh did not just provide sub-sistence. Many wetland products could also be sold. Defoe documented how entrepreneurial Fennish were even selling fresh fish to the capital: 'Here is a particular trade carried on with London ... Carrying fish ... by land carriage; this they do by carrying great butts filled with water in wagons ... The butts have a little square flap, instead of a bung ... and every night, when they come to the inn, they draw off the water, and let more fresh and sweet water run into them again.'[18]

Peat, eels, game, feathers, hay, and dairy products were other products of the fen that found a ready market. The demand for reed (it was much longer-lasting than straw as a roofing mater-ial) grew fast during the population growth of the eighteenth century. In the deepest fen grew the particularly valuable giant saw-sedge *Cladium mariscus*, highly sought after as a capping ridge as it could keep out rain for generations. Various other wild plants were harvested and sold for bedding, baskets and clogs. Pollard willows were cut and sold for poles, baskets, wood and firewood in a seven- to ten-year rotation cycle.[19]

As the proportion of the English population dependent on wages grew, the demand for hemp clothing increased. Hemp, which could be seasonally grown in the common fields that flooded in winter, was the basis for the spinning and weav-ing industry that provided a significant source of income for women through their 'hempensun' (the origin of 'homespun') cloth.[20]

Self-sufficiency supplemented by cash sales from the nat-ural resources of the common allowed the Fennish to adapt successfully to the market economy emerging in early modern England. In the first half of the eighteenth century, this was *not* an indigenous culture in terminal decline. Those who sought to enclose the Fens spoke a truth when they described drainage as being about transforming the land *and* the people. They understood as well as the Fennish themselves, that the destruction of the common marsh would take away the economic independence on which the people's freedom relied.

The successful defence of a large part of the Fens meant that the region became an increasingly important refuge for transient people being evicted from more strictly policed and successfully enclosed regions of England. In particular, the widely-persecuted Roma seem to have had an accepted place in Fennish society. In the nineteenth century, W.B. Stonehouse documented one family's long connection with the Isle of Axholme:

A gang of gypsies generally called Boswells from one Charles Boswell of Rossington ... have frequented the lanes and commons of the Isle ... from time immemorial ... Charles Boswell was buried at Rossington in the year 1708 or 1709. He is still remembered in the traditions of the villagers as having established a species of sovereignty over that singular people ...[21]

The Boswells roamed well beyond the Isle. When Moses, son of Aaron and Matilda Boswell, was baptised in Horbling on 24 April 1825, his family was described as 'travellers', not 'strangers' or 'paupers' as other transient people were.[22] The Boswells maintain their connection to the Lincolnshire fens through to this day, as documented by the museum established by one of Charles' descendants.*

The place of fringe-dwellers who lived in family groups deep in the marsh also seems to have been accepted. The nineteenth-century Boston engineer and local historian, W.H. Wheeler, documented how:

> In isolated spots, scattered over the low, flooded fen part, lived the Fen Slodgers ... who got their living by fishing and fowling ... These men were violently opposed to any attempts to alter the state of the Fens, believing they had a kind of vested interest in the fishing and fowling, by which they gained their scanty subsistence. Although their condition was very miserable, they nevertheless enjoyed a sort of wild liberty amidst the watery wastes, which they were not disposed to give up.[23]

It is likely that the 'slodgers' had a community policing or neighbourhood watch role – monitoring, protecting and defending resources in areas that were beyond the easy reach and eyes of the villagers. In return for access to food and other resources, they became front-line defenders of the common.

* The Boswell Romany Museum, established by Gordon Boswell, is in Clay Lake, Spalding, Lincolnshire.

In the summer, some presumably also became 'drovers' – charged with looking after cattle on the common pastures and impounding animals illegitimately placed there.

The Fennish were also capable of excluding outsiders, both to manage the common resource and out of fear. As Steve Hindle has shown in his review of the vestry minute books of Frampton and nine other Holland Fen parishes, prejudice to poor migrants could be marked and even extended to prohibitions of marriages. Those charged with administering relief saw their legal and moral obligations to be confined to people long settled in the parish.[24] This system of aid could work reasonably well when people stayed in their home villages, but as dispossession intensified across England due to enclosure, the Fens – the largest and richest lowland common in the nation – became a powerful magnet for the upwards of 10 per cent of the English population who were now paupers.[25] While the benefits of industrialisation were slowly shared after 1850, before this time dispossession frequently meant intergenerational hunger and homelessness for former commoners. In this context it is not surprising that thousands of refugees flocked to the Fens, and while some found a new home in the marsh, others were vilified and harassed until they moved on to who knows where.

The pressures on the land and the culture of its custodians during the eighteenth century were real, but it is a testimony to the resilience of the environment and its people that the Fennish flourished in this period of rapid change. Far from being inevitably destroyed by the rise of a capitalist economy, the common conferred competitive advantages within it. The main reason that this vitality is often missed is because of persistent misunderstandings concerning what 'the common' actually was.

CHAPTER 11

Body, Mind and Spirit

What was the 'common' that was so fiercely defended by the Fennish? Did it *only* mean access to the economic resources of a bountiful marsh?

R.H. Tawney, the most influential social historian of the first half of the twentieth century, observed that the commons 'reposed upon a common custom and tradition, not upon documentary records capable of precise construction'.[1] Customary rights and responsibilities were highly localised, with ancient origins that were rarely written down. The widespread assumption that the common can be equated with a legal right to access land and resources hides the reality, majesty and mystery of the commoners' world. The judgements of enclosure commissioners and courts worked on the principle established since the Norman conquest that all of England was owned by the monarch or by those on whom the Crown had conferred a property right. But in much of the Fens – where the reach of monarchical and lordly power was constrained by water and mud – ancient customary practices, closer in spirit and practice to tribal tradition than modern property law, survived well into the eighteenth century.

Customary use did have a legal standing but to establish it there was a need to show the court that not only had there been a continuity in practice, but that this had been unchanged over time. Customs which adapted to changing environmental and economic conditions were not considered customs at all, meaning the vitality of indigenous culture could be employed to undermine the legal legitimacy of common right. The codification of 'custom', as much as a disregard for it, threatened the commons.

The complex 'intercommoning' system, by which different villages shared the custodianship of a wetland, is evidence for the pre-Norman roots of the Fens commons. As the Royal Commissioners who investigated the common lands of England during the 1950s found, 'intercommoning by several villages is older than manorial organisation, which was superimposed at a later date'. They believed that intercommoning can be traced to the 'great customary grazing grounds' in which 'common rights had no need of definition' because they were based on 'customary practices'.[2]

To understand the meaning of the common, it is thus important not to confuse ancient and ever-evolving customary use with specified 'customary' legal rights. The next challenge is to grapple with the difference between a modern and an indigenous way of being.

The commons was as much a series of interwoven and dynamic relationships with people and place as it was a system of land management. The sharp distinction between self, community and land that is now embedded in the western mind did not exist in the Fennish world. An indigenous identity rooted in belonging is a difficult concept to convey because it is now taken for granted that the individual exists independently of society and environment. By contrast, when John Manwood attempted to define the common in 1598 he put the emphasis on *relationships*: 'It taketh the name of Common, a Communitate, of communitie, participation, or fellowship, because that most commonly, where men have common of pasture for the feeding of their beastes or cattell, many mens cattell do use to feedde there together.'[3] In more recent times, poetry, such as that written by John Clare in the nineteenth century, has perhaps come closest to conveying the relational ties that characterised a world in which 'all life's little crowd /That haunt the waters, fields and woods' shared 'nature's wide and common sky'.[4]

A commoner's daily existence was enmeshed in social ties that were inseparable from the country they inhabited. As Nicola Whyte has documented, it 'was through the practical knowledge of the landscape, through the memory of the past and the ongoing physical experience of living and working in a particular place, that people defined their social and economic identities'. The land was 'not simply an economic resource: it was infused with layers of spiritual, social and cultural meaning'.[5]

Individual freedom of choice in the contemporary sense ('to be who you choose to be') could not be imagined, but the mutual obligations that defined daily life and provided support in child rearing, ageing, sickness, disability and death, conferred another sort of freedom – one entwined in interdependence and belonging.[6]

The commons were also the ground for cultural practice and ritual. The resources of the marsh fostered a work cycle that reinforced communal relations and celebrated nature's fecundity. Activities from egg-gathering to fishing were done in groups according to nature's predictable timetable. June was the start of the peat-cutting, which went on into October; and late June and July was the season to cut bulrushes. Reed was cut in winter.[7]

Religious festivals marked nature's calendar. On Trinity Monday, Mildenhall commoners entered the fen to take sedge and thatch, while common grazing there occurred between the Feast of St Peter and the Feast of the Purification of Our Lady (commonly called Candlemas). As in other places, the saint days that survived the Reformation were those most closely linked to the cycle of common rights. Even the diminished Protestant calendar continued to mark the opening and closing of shared pastures through celebrations on Lammas Day (Feast of St Peter) on 1 August, Michaelmas (Feast of the Archangel) on 29 September, and Martinmas (Feast of St Martin) on 11 November.[8]

The celebration of saints' days was one dimension of the spiritual connection to land. The Fennish were Christian and a role for the Church was accepted, but the institution's usual rural authority, dependent as it was on an alliance with lord and state, was limited by the freedom provided by the common. The anonymous author of the eighteenth-century poem (who described himself as a 'Fen Parson'), *The Inundation or The Life of a Fen-Man*, noted that fenmen 'rarely resort' to 'parish churches … unless to a wedding, a christening, or a burying'.[9] This was the same complaint that Samuel Wesley made in the Isle of Axholme, where on his reckoning less than 1 per cent of the population attended the communion service he offered each month.[10]

It is likely that the Reformation was partly responsible for diluting the connection between the Fennish and the Church. Many of the remote communities were serviced in the medieval period by a chapel – subsidiaries of the parish church that were largely closed during the sixteenth century (becoming ruins, barns or, in the case of the chapel of St Mary in Walpole Fen, a cottage) as the official focus of religious piety was concentrated in the village church. In terms of the sacred landscape, more significant still was the loss of the hermitages, priories, standing crosses and shrines formerly linked to monastic establishments, saints and pilgrimage routes (including the different paths to the shrine at Walsingham, one of which went through King's Lynn).[11] It is well documented that the Protestant triumph curtailed and controlled the religious imagination but perhaps in remote regions like the Fens, it also liberated it. Certainly, many isolated communities were largely left to their own devices until non-conformist chapels filled the void left by the apathy of the state Church during the nineteenth century.

During the seventeenth and eighteenth centuries, with four or five parishes often sharing a minister and holy communion rarely held, the Church of England did not try very hard to influence the spiritual life of the Fennish. This neglect angered Arthur Young, for whom 'improvement' was as much about improving morals as agricultural output. He argued that 'National prosperity depends on the industry of the common people; industry on good morals; and … good morals amongst the poor are nursed only by the Gospel being preached to them'. Young worried that without religious instruction or the honouring of the Sabbath, people would be rendered 'savages'. 'I know nothing', he memorably concluded (before his mind was changed by witnessing post-enclosure poverty), 'better calculated to fill a country with barbarians ready for any mischief, than extensive commons, and divine service only once a month.'[12]

As Young's pleas to the elite suggest, the attack on the commons was partly justified by attacking commoner 'superstitions'. Those targeted in the civilising mission of enclosure included 'witches': women healers, herbalists and spiritual guides whose authority was rooted in traditions that reflected the co-existence of Christian and pre-Christian ideas.[13] Romany women were particularly highly regarded as healers. For the common people, there was no tension between Christianity and these older ways of understanding the physical and spiritual world. It was dualistic post-Reformation churchmen for whom belief in apparitions such as Will o' the Wisps

St Guthlac sailing to Crowland (*Life of St Guthlac*, 12th century).
(Culture Club/Getty Images)

'East End of Crowland Abbey', from *Our Own Country*, Vol. I (1898).
(The Print Collector/Getty Images)

Ely Cathedral, ca. 1910.
(Archivist/Alamy Stock Photo)

St Botolph's Church, Boston.
(Rod Edwards/Alamy Stock Photo)

The rescue of the young John Wesley from the fire
that destroyed Epworth rectory, 1709.
(Granger, NYC/Alamy Stock Photo)

A windmill with Ely Cathedral in the background (1887 engraving).
(benoitb/Getty Images)

Francis, 4th Earl
of Bedford.
(ART Collection/
Alamy Stock Photo)

William, 5th Earl
of Bedford.
(Classic Image/
Alamy Stock Photo)

A skeleton pump of the type used to drain the Norfolk Fens (dated 19th century).
(World History Archive/Alamy Stock Photo)

Drainage of Whittlesey Mere – the dyke-cutting, 1851 (*Illustrated London News*).
(Antiqua Print Gallery/Alamy Stock Photo)

Holme Lode in the 19th century before it was drained.

(Hilary Morgan/Alamy Stock Photo)

Skating match at Littleport, 1891 (*Illustrated London News*).

(Antiqua Print Gallery/Alamy Stock Photo)

East Yorkshire wildfowler Snowden Slights in a punt
with his punt gun (early 20th century).
(Historic Collection/Alamy Stock Photo)

'Throwing the hood', Haxey, 1953.
(Keystone Pictures USA/Alamy Stock Photo)

Stacking reed for thatch, Wicken Fen, 1950s.
(Chronicle/Alamy Stock Photo)

Wetlands at Wicken Fen, 2019.
(Andrew Michael/Alamy Stock Photo)

(mysterious lights that might have their origins in spontaneous combustion of marsh gas) and other mystical phenomena was just pagan superstition.[14]

The Fennish had their own mythical figures to complement the rich mythology of the local Celtic saints. In the novel *The Manuscript of the Red Box*, the hero, Frank Vavasour, goes into hiding at the 'Lindholme Hermitage'. This is a reference to 'Billy Lindum', the hermit who was reputed to have lived on a small island of Hatfield Moor, and who became a character in many local stories.[15]

Tom Hickathrift, a giant-killer who defended Fennish lands, was another celebrated figure. John Weever's *Ancient Funeral Monuments* (1631) states that the origins of the Hickathrift legend go back to a time when conflict broke out between local people and those wanting to enclose 1,200 acres of pasture known as 'The Smeeth' – a common shared by seven villages. Tom's job was to cart beer for a King's Lynn brewer, and this required him to drive his cart across the contested common. Seeing the locals 'faint-hearted and ready to take flight', Tom 'set upon the ... adversaries of the Common [and] encouraged his neighbours to go forward and fight valiantly in defence of their liberties'. The local people then 'chased the landlord and his company to the utmost verge of the said Common; which from that time they have quietly enjoyed to this very day.' In 1657, the antiquarian William Dugdale reported seeing the grave of this hero: 'At the east end of Tilney chancel in the churchyard is a grave stone, about eight foot in length, which they report to be the Tombstone of one Hickofrix, who encountered a Giant with a Cart wheel for his shield, and the Axtree for his weapon ... and overcame the same Giant, as the tale goes.'[16] Perhaps this stone was a place of local pilgrimage and devotion given that, as Maureen James notes, in some stories Tom continued to defend the fen from invaders even after his death.[17]

Storytelling could be facilitated by the powers of the opium poppy. The dried residue obtained from the juice of the flowers was chewed and their heads drunk in tea to relieve malaria and promote wellbeing for centuries before imperial expansion saw large quantities of the drug imported into England from India, when notorious dens opened in London and port cities. In the nineteenth century, although patches of white poppies remained a feature of Fenland gardens for personal use, this foreign product was marketed and abused in a way that was alien to traditional life. In 1846, the Lincoln *Mercury* warned that the 'the practice of taking opium, laudanum, ether and morphine has increased and is increasing amongst the population of the fens of Cambridgeshire and Lincolnshire to a frightful extent'. In the 1860s, the travel writer Walter White recorded that 'One thing is certain, opium-eating for medicinal purposes prevails largely in the fens' and 'opium-chewing has become a habit as well as necessity'. He observed that if you 'stand in a druggist's shop in the fens on a market day, you would see many a farmer's wife and many a rustic labourer enter and lay down their pence for a small packet of opium'.[18] The most popular preparations were known as laudanum, which was an alcoholic herbal mixture containing 10 per cent opium. The notorious 'Godfrey's Cordial', colloquially termed 'mother's friend' because it was used to get babies to sleep, was the most heavily promoted brand.[19] In the post-enclosure era, when women were forced into the casual labour market to feed their families, a sleeping baby became an economic necessity. As late as the 1970s, an elderly woman from Isleham near Ely recalled that as a child she worked alongside women in the fields who 'had their babies on their backs and they'd give them a little bit of laudanum on sugar to keep them asleep'. She thought 'most women did that – especially when they was binding, because they was working for the Master, so their children had to be kept quiet then. Sometimes they gave them too much.'[20] Though opium's addictive qualities were not fully understood, the misuse of the drug was an example of the problem experienced by many indigenous cultures when a traditional mind-altering substance, formerly controlled by custom, was commodified in a market economy.

Opium was not the only treatment for 'ague'. John Wesley recalled other cures from growing up in the Isle of Axholme in his bestselling book *Primitive Physic*. In letter to a friend, Wesley recorded that he believed that 'one or other of the remedies against ague ... will hardly fail. I depend most on 1. The [opium based] pills. If these fail, 2. On the *sal prunellae*. If that fail, 3. On the spirits of hartshorn.'*[21]

---

* *Sal prunella* is an impure potassium carbonate obtained from the ashes of wormwood. 'Spirits of hartshorn' is a solution of ammonia in water that in Wesley's time was obtained from distilled hartshorn shavings.

The commons was also a place of play. While the line between leisure and work was not distinct, the Fennish did gather for set-aside days of celebration. The most famous of these involved games of Fen football that were commonly referred to as 'camping'. England had many different forms of football before rules were standardised, but given that a precursor to the modern game was the one codified at Cambridge University, it is likely that Fennish football played an important role in the origins of the game we know today (just as the folk football played by the people of Rugby influenced the game played at Rugby School).

In Fen football, two or more villages gathered and played in an open area. The 'field' could be miles long, and, although the rules were unclear to outside observers, those who concluded that 'anything goes' were almost certainly wrong. Even today, people watching rugby, or Irish or Australian forms of football without any familiarity with the game can have a similar reaction. No doubt for Fennish participants and spectators, the rules were clear enough.

Accounts of football being played in the Fens date back to the Middle Ages, and it is well documented how the Fennish used gathering for a game as a cover to organise during periods of resistance. For example, in June 1638, hundreds of people from the Littleport area assembled in Whelpmore and Burnt Fen to play at camping, and then destroyed the new ditches being dug to drain the common marsh.[22]

In the 1920s, Christopher Marlowe documented other traditional games and ritualised practices still surviving in the

Fens, such as 'Throwing the Hood' at Haxey, and the Feast of St Owen at Haddenham. These had been practised since pagan times.[23]

Gathering for games and festivals was facilitated by the fact that the homeland of the Fennish was, by pre-industrial standards, an easily traversed one. Far from being a barrier to communication, water made it easy to get about, once hidden landmarks were known. Sometimes stilts and drain poles were needed to vault over water, but even this form of transport sped up movement for skilled users, rather than slowed it down. Roads also existed for those with the eyes to see them. The famous one that ran from Boston to the high country via the West Fen was called the Nordyke and Hilldyke Causeway. Because the track was only distinguishable by rows of willows emerging from water, this was a perilous journey for strangers, but for the local guides employed to take people across, the way forward was clear.[24]

The successful defence of so much of the common meant that in 1700 the Fens were not just the last large 'untamed' region of lowland England in an ecological sense but in a human one too. The Fennish comprised the largest group of English people still to be brought under effective state, ecclesiastical, landlord and employer control. James C. Scott argues that the move to a reliance on agriculture alone 'represented a contraction of our species' attention to and practical knowledge of the natural world, a contraction of diet, a contraction of space, and perhaps a contraction as well in the breadth of ritual life'.[25] When we compare Fennish cultural life in their wetland common with that of the daily grind of the agricultural workers in the landscape that replaced it, the truth in Scott's observation can be seen.

The Fennish, like most indigenous cultures, left few written records. This means that the best measure we have of their connection to community and country remains the depth of their resistance to drainage and enclosure. Before 1750, defeating thousands of indigenous people fighting to defend their homeland had proved to be a near-impossible task. But in the late eighteenth century, the balance of power would shift because of the growing might of an increasingly militarised and centralised state.

CHAPTER 12

The Triumph of the Imperial State

During the eighteenth century, the new nation of Britain expanded its geographic reach, achieving effective control of the Scottish Highlands and Ireland, as well as expanding its realms in North America, India and the Caribbean. The expansion of empire was contemporaneous with the extension of state power within England itself. Indeed, New England was colonised *before* the marshlands adjacent to the Fens port of Boston from where the Pilgrim Fathers departed.

The power available to the government to impose its will internally and externally was increased by the development of a standing army from 1660 as well as the range of new laws enacted in the early eighteenth century.[1] The most infamous of these, the so-called Black Act, provided a wide range of punishment options, including the death penalty, for over 50 flexibly-defined offences. While the catalyst for the legislation had been poaching by men with blackened faces said to be Jacobites, the Bill targeted anyone involved in protest impacting on private property and political privilege. The fact that people could now be executed or transported for so many offences (including arson – the traditional last-resort protest option) was intended to deter those who might be tempted to fight back against poverty and dispossession.[2]

New laws, a professional army, consolidated internal power and more sophisticated state institutions meant that, after 1760, the commoners faced an increasingly powerful central government that was determined to win the fight for the Fens.

The attack on the Fennish was part of an extraordinary national effort, unique in Europe, to enclose common lands by decree. Between 1750 and 1820, 21 per cent of England or 6.8 million acres was enclosed by an Act of Parliament.[3] Between 1760 and 1800 alone there were 1,800 separate enclosure bills, scores of which related to the Fens. But these laws would have meant little without the capacity to implement them. Critical to the 'success' of the legislation was the ability of an emboldened central government to assert its will through punishment, retribution and force.

Some enclosure laws and processes were fairer than others (much depended on the paid commissioners appointed to oversee them) and almost all provided some compensation in land or cash to those who could prove a common right. However, many people, including most women and those without provable property ties, lacked any defined right and were excluded from the process altogether. As John Maynard, the probable author of the anonymous pamphlet, *The Anti-Projector: Or The History of the Fen Project*, had argued over a hundred years before, here were 'many thousand cottagers which live in our fens, which otherwise must go a begging'.[4] Such people enjoyed a customary access to the resources of the Fen (they were not trespassers and were connected to the community) but few proved to have a legal one.

Horbling Fen was the one of the first of the commons of southern Lincolnshire to be enclosed by statute. The 1764 Act 'for Dividing and Inclosing the open and Common Fields, Meadows and Common Fen in the Parish of Horbling' led to the loss of 1,353 acres of wetland.[5] This enclosure is well researched because at the height of the Second World War, W.H. Hosford from the School of Continuing Education at University College (now the University of Nottingham) took a class of Workers' Educational Association students to Horbling. In his report on the class, Hosford recorded that:

> A firm of solicitors established in the village since the eighteenth Century – possibly the only firm of solicitors situated in a village – was able to produce a number of documents relating to the Horbling enclosure, and some other legal enclosures, and these were very kindly lent to the tutor. Some of the students made prolonged researches into parish records and produced information upon such points as the extent to which former common-right holders remained in the village after enclosure and died there; the numbers who were in receipt of poor-relief after the enclosure; changes in the poor rates after the enclosure and facilities for poorer persons to keep cows after the extinction of the common.[6]

The students also documented resistance to the enclosure. One man would not sign the relevant documents because 'he thrt it wd. Hu[r]t the poor'. A woman refused to do so because 'as she was old she had rather things remained as they were'.[7]

Most with an identified common right *did* sign the Horbling agreement. However, the majority of these beneficiaries turned out to be not resident in the village at all. It seems that land speculators, mostly merchants, professional men and landowners of Boston and London, had been buying up land in the village prior to enclosure. Their strategy was a simple one – purchase property in the expectation of capital gain and then promote enclosure to realise it.[8]

The appointed commissioners determined that at the time of enclosure, common rights in Horbling were only attached to fifteen farm houses, five houses, and 44 cottages. The large majority of residents rented their property, but Hosford found that in this instance at least 'the Legislature and the Commissioners were concerned only with the proprietors ... they were not in any way concerned with the tenants'.[9] Nevertheless, active resistance to the enclosure of the fen around Horbling, as far as now can be ascertained, was limited. But this would not prove to be the case elsewhere.

The enclosure of the wetland around Boston was initiated by the Witham Act of 1762. This legislation prompted the construction of a new Grand Sluice in Boston to replace the one destroyed in the protests of 1653, with its gala opening in 1766 signalling the capacity and intent to enclose the surrounding country. The push was driven by the two biggest potential beneficiaries of enclosure, Lord Monson and the Earl of Stamford.

A public meeting at Sleaford's Angel Inn in August 1766 voted to proceed with developing an enclosure bill to take to Parliament. A second meeting in October at the same venue (for which there was actually time to prepare) objected to this plan, but the proponents pushed on regardless.[10]

A petition requesting enclosure was presented to the House of Commons on 4 December 1766 and leave was given to Lord Robert Bertie, Lord George Sackville, and Lord Brownlow Bertie to prepare and introduce a Bill. The legislation was read for the first time five days later. On 4 March 1767 a long petition against the enclosure was presented and the signatories included Trinity College, Cambridge (which had common rights arising from its ownership of property in the former Gilbertine-owned fen village of Swineshead). Nevertheless, the Bill was read for second time on 6 March 1767, prompting further petitions for and against its passing.[11]

The Enclosure Bill limited those with a commoner right to those who paid tax on property. The result was that only 614 persons were deemed to be commoners. Because many of these were not residents it is difficult to be certain what proportion of local people had any say in the process – but it was probably less than 10 per cent. Of the 614, there were supposedly 94 objectors, 53 who could not be located, 40 indifferent, and 427 who agreed to enclosure. But these figures disguise the level of opposition. The Bill stated that a 75 per cent majority was needed to prevent enclosure, with this to be measured not by the numbers of people but by the tax they paid. It is thus very likely that some people who opposed change recognised that lodging a protest vote would achieve nothing except to antagonise the powerful proponents on which their future livelihoods might depend. The vote for enclosure was an entirely predictable outcome.[12]

Royal assent to the Enclosure Bill was granted on 29 June 1767, with the commissioners appointed soon after. Their first job was to clear the marshland of all human presence. Weirs, fishing nets, eel traps, jetties, boats, shacks, various artefacts and dwellings were removed or destroyed, and residents evicted from their 'illegal' homes.[13]

To pay the expenses associated with the clearances, the commissioners auctioned off areas of higher land mostly near the villages, with the result that many more people were evicted from their homes, and rents went up for those who remained. People were given only a month to find the money to purchase their land before it was auctioned. Some mortgages were reclaimed to prevent householders from bidding at all. Others found their affordable long-term lease replaced by an expensive short one. A local play, *Brothertoft Ablaze*, and John Thomas Bealby's novel *Daughter of the Fen* remember the suffering that came with eviction.[14]

The 'slodgers' – those who lived within the wetland without any defined claim – suffered the most. Their livelihood and homes were wantonly destroyed without notice or any consideration of compensation. Clearing out 'squatters' was presented as a contribution to public order and safety.

Shock at the scale and speed of enclosure most likely limited the initial resistance. But as the conquest accelerated, the fightback began.

On 6 June 1768, several hundred protesters assembled at Hubbards Bridge and marched three miles to Boston. There they confronted the solicitor, Edward Draper, and forced him to hand over the enclosure papers – which they ripped up and threw into the street. They then moved on to Robert Barlow's home and threatened to wreck his house if he refused to sign a paper declaring he would never again promote enclosure. He signed. The Fennish then proceeded to Frampton and successfully made the same demand on two more men.[15]

It was at this point that the expansion of the enforcement powers available to the government since the failed drainage attempt a hundred years before became evident. The authorities immediately brought in four troops of Royal Scots Greys. The origins of this legendary cavalry regiment of the British army went back to the late seventeenth century. Although they were the veterans of various continental campaigns, by this time the troops were exclusively employed for policing duties within Britain itself.

The soldiers were permanently stationed in Boston and its surrounds to protect the property of those promoting enclosure and the men undertaking the works. The landowners also raised their own militia but the Scots Greys' commander ordered them to disband. This enclosure was to proceed according to law and be enforced by the military acting on the orders of the central government.

Despite the imbalance in firepower, the British army would find (as they did elsewhere in the empire) that it was still not easy to defeat people fighting for home and country. The term 'guerrilla war' would not be used until the early nineteenth century, but this form of warfare had been employed in the Fens since at least the Roman invasion and was now adopted again with great effect. Who was the fighter and who was the fisherman or farmer? Boundaries blur when ordinary homes become barracks and whole communities uphold a strict code of silence. When in early 1769 all boundary posts, rails, and hedges associated with the drainage were destroyed, the authorities simply had no way of identifying who was responsible.[16]

The strength gained from the stories of the past should also not be underestimated. Accounts of the successful resistance of a century before must have been recounted and embellished around hearth and home for generations. People fought for the sake of their children *and* their ancestors.

So extensive was the destruction of property that an Act of Parliament was passed in 1770 to amend the original enclosure legislation to allow boundaries to be marked by wide ditches instead of vulnerable fences and hedges. This Bill also set aside £1,000 to prosecute offenders and pay rewards to those providing information. The Corporation of Boston initiated a number of these legal actions, forcing the resistance to become even more covert. Fire was now widely employed despite arson being a capital offence, with barns and haystacks burnt and stock killed.[17]

One of the resistance leaders, William Smith of Swineshead, was known as 'Gentleman Smith'. Tradition has it that he gambled away his inheritance and was forced to mortgage the family estate, the mortgage holders foreclosing before he could profit from enclosure. As a result of this injustice, Smith changed his allegiance and joined the protesters. However, caution is needed in the emphasis placed on Smith's leadership role. Conquering elites throughout the British empire were prone to exaggerate the importance of an educated turncoat in promoting indigenous resistance; the 'trouble' stirred up by such men being a preferable explanation for the malice of local people than injustice.

Initially the fightback focused on the property and animals of active enclosure proponents. Two Boston-based men had their coach horses poisoned and a Frampton resident had 50 sheep hamstrung. W. Watson of Kirton was warned that his house would be demolished if he promoted further enclosures. This strategy had some impact. John Parkinson of Asgarby wrote that: 'No gentleman on the spot cares to be the entire Promoter of so extensive an Improvement … on account of seeing the Holland Fen Inclosure executed, in which those who were called Advocates either suffered by having their Stacks fired or such other Private damages which might be as injurious as the Advantages any Individual might Receive.'[18]

The problem for the Fennish was that most of the principal beneficiaries of the enclosure did not live anywhere near the fen. Secure in distant citadels, they employed the power of the courts and the state, the skills of well-paid contractors and the muscle of conscripted labour, to progress their conquest. This meant that in 1768, as conflict intensified, armed resistance cells began to target all collaborators under the cover of darkness. John Woods, a Swineshead farmer, was shot dead by his fireside, while a failed attempt on Robert Barlow's life resulted in the shooting and wounding of his wife. Thomas Wilkes, a bailiff at Brothertoft, was shot in the face through a window shutter, lost an eye and was 'dreadfully disfigured'. In July 1769 at a farm in Algarkirk Fen, assailants were shot at and one member of the resistance was killed before the others fled.[19]

On the night of 27 July 1769, John Yerburgh had his house attacked. The *London Gazette* reported that:

> some evil disposed Person or Persons unknown did maliciously shoot into the dwelling-House of Mr John Yerburgh, at Frampton ... with a Gun or other Fire-Arms, loaded with Sluggs, which damaged the said House; and a threatening Letter was afterwards found in the Court-Yard of the said House ... which contained the Words and Letters following, viz. 'John Yar Brah this is to let you know that As you have used the Utmost of your power to persuade your Neighbours and knaves like your Self to Cheat the Poor of their Right Except a Reformation is heard of in the neighbourhood that but the beginning of Sorrow from your frind and wel wisher to Liberty & an open fen for Ever'.[20]

Much of the violence on both sides was never documented. In July 1833, the Stamford *Mercury* reported the unearthing of human remains buried in a barrel of lime in an orchard at Kirton Holme. One local remembered that Lineham, a local poet 'well acquainted with the persons and proceedings of the rioters', was suddenly missed and probably murdered in fear that he, or his songs, would betray those involved in the actions.[21] But wasn't it more likely that this ballad-maker of the resistance, whose poems celebrated the fight and named-up the oppressors, had been killed by the other side?

What is clear is that no one was ever prosecuted for the killings. There were, though, a number of successful prosecutions for the destruction of property, with those identified or randomly picked out from the crowd enduring hefty fines and prison terms. The Black Act was used in 1769 to charge James Rylatt of Swineshead for shooting cattle and burning fence posts in the Holland Fen enclosures of Charles Anderson Pelham, lord of the manor of Earlshall-in-Frampton.[22]

But the legal process was expensive. On 23 September 1772, the resilient Boston solicitor Edward Draper presented his account for expenses incurred in 'prosecuting the persons concerned in the late riots and disturbances' and claimed the extraordinary sum of £1,473 (equivalent to over £270,000 in 2020).[23]

The role played by the state in enclosure was not confined to laws, courts and the deployment of soldiers. Robert Carter, a disaffected landowner in north Lincolnshire, wrote a pamphlet in 1772 which argued that, far from being an example of the power of the free market, from Barton to Broughton works were 'done on private estates at the public expense'. Carter believed that the process was being decided not according to the public good but according to 'the weight of Favouritism, Power and Interest'.[24]

Carter's defence of the river he colloquially called the 'Redbourn' (after his home village of Redbourne, near what is more usually known as the River Ancholme) captures something of the depth of belonging that drainage disrupted:

> Alas Poor Redbourn! What hast thou ever done to provoke the Rage and Malice of thy enemies against Thee! … Alas! Friendship, Honour, Justice, Truth must all fall a Sacrifice to the Altars of Interest. Thou didn't never stir out of thy peaceful Domains to disturb and invade the Possessions of others, and to impose Laws and Taxes upon them which they were not able to bear, pretending to know their Interest, Situation and circumstances better than their Possessors … Redbourn meets not with one Friend or Advocate in the House of Commons to defend it from Wrong … Though thou hast always contented thyself in cultivating thy (by Nature) too barren Fields … yet from hence the Neighbouring Poor were cloathed, and the Hungry fed … [until] a most cruel spoiler came and at one Stroke robbed thee of all the Fruits of thy Labour … But where interest is the ruling passion, and Rage to increase estates, expectations of redress are chimerical.[25]

Carter made the point that the drainage commissioners did not recognise the critical role played by flooding in *maintaining* fertility and that they overlooked the significant impact of small-scale local drainage work in mitigating the worst effects of winter waters. Whatever view is taken on the worth of the large engineering projects undertaken by the commissioners, there is no doubt that customary knowledge was ignored by those who profited from the total transformation of the landscape.

Carter had good reason to conclude that the enclosure and drainage of his fen was less about increasing production than appropriating its wealth. Whether enclosure increased total economic output is unclear, but there is no doubt that it increased the share going to large landowners.

It was mid-June 1773, five years after armed protest began, before resistance to drainage and enclosure significantly reduced in the Lincolnshire fens. By this time, the landscape had been radically altered. Stark, muddy fields full of rotten decaying matter had replaced the once bounteous marsh. This sight must have produced widespread despair and made further resistance seem futile.

It is difficult to document how the transformation of the land impacted on the psychology and spirit of its people. But it is interesting that a number of southern Lincolnshire men who grew up at this time – Matthew Flinders, George Bass and John Franklin among them – became explorers and colonisers. Did their wandering have anything to do with the fact that in their formative years they had borne witness to a new country replacing the old?

After the enclosure of Holland Fen was complete, the move to enclose the remaining fens still surrounding it began. A petition to Parliament in 1780 attempted to halt this by detailing the beauty and fecundity of the East Fen:

> It is a vast tract of morass, intermixed with numbers of lakes, from half a mile to two or three miles in circuit, communicating with each other by narrow reedy straits. They are very shallow, none above four or five feet deep, but abound with pike, perch, ruffs, bream, tench, dace, eels, etc. The reeds which cover the Fens are cut annually for thatching not only cottages, but many good houses. The multitude of stares [starlings] that roost in these reeds in winter break down many by perching on them ... the birds which inhabit the different Fens are very numerous. Besides the common wild duck, wild geese, garganies, pochards, shovellers, and teals breed here, pewit, gulls, and black terns abound ... The great crested grebe, called gaunts, are found in the East fen. The lesser-crested grebe, the black and dusky and the little grebe, cootes, water-hens, and spotted water-hens, water rails, ruffs, red-shanks, lapwings or wypes, red-breasted godwits, and whimbrels are inhabitants of these Fens.[26]

A 1784 petition made a further plea to Parliament that 'many of us, by the blessing of God and our own industry, has procured a cow or two, which we graze in the said fen in the summer, and get fodder for their support in the winter', but:

> of these privileges we are great measure deprived by a set of men called Commissioners, who hath imbibed such a rage for drainage, that exceeds both utility and justice. Utility, because it destroys the grass and herbage, and is hurtful both to its farmers and poor men; justice because it deprives the poor of their privileges – for the fishery is ruined, the thatch is destroyed and the fodder very scarce.[27]

These petitions were ignored and in 1801 legislation was passed for the enclosure of the East and West Fens.[28]

The long fight against the French and the fear of food shortages that resulted from this, meant that Bills to enclose nearly all the remaining fen commons passed Parliament with almost no debate during this period. On any judgement (including that of Arthur Young and more compassionate supporters of enclosure), the compensation provided to the poor was inadequate. When Marham in Norfolk was enclosed in 1807, only 200 acres were allocated to the poor from the 4,000 acres of rich common that had formerly sustained its 799 inhabitants. This was generous compared to nearby Shouldham, population 725, where 100 acres were allocated to the poor out of a marshland common of 3,775 acres. Commissioners did not even require that enclosed parcels of land were farmed. In Shouldham, a large area of the former common became a private rabbit warren owned by Sir Thomas

Hare. While down the road at Hilgay, the 166 acres set aside at the time of enclosure for the poor was soon rented out for £135 to offset the poor rates meant to be paid by landowners to sustain the growing number of the destitute.[29]

How did the dispossessed Fennish survive? Some found permanent work on enclosed farms where dependence on waged labour meant a new level of subservience. Generally though, rural people didn't move into secure jobs but seasonal, unreliable, and precarious work. Much of this in the early and mid-nineteenth century was done by gangs. The Sixth (and last) Report of the Children's Employment Commission, published at the end of March 1867, documented the reality of the new labour market. The Commission found that a gang system was particularly common in the former fenlands of Lincolnshire. Karl Marx quoted its findings in *Capital*:

> The gang consist of 10 to 40 or 50 persons, women, young persons of both sexes ... and children of both sexes (6–13 years of age). At the head is the gang-master, always an ordinary agricultural labourer ... He is the recruiting sergeant for the gang, which works under him, not under the farmer. He generally arranges with the latter for piece work, and his income ... depends almost entirely upon the dexterity with which he manages to extract within the shortest time the greatest possible amount of labour from his gang.[30]

Other former commoners were forced to move to towns and cities where there was work in factories, ports and new industries, or survive as best as they could on the streets. Some became colonisers themselves in distant parts of the growing empire.[31] Others took to the laneways to join the growing group of vagrants wandering England at this time – their life made difficult by new vagrancy laws that made begging illegal and homelessness a crime.

A measure of post-enclosure poverty is the number of people receiving emergency aid from the parish. In Frampton near Boston, only £80 was spent on poor relief in the 1740s. During the 1790s it was £312.[32]

By 1830 the Fens was a very different place from 50 years before. William Cobbett described Holbeach on his tour through the Fens in spring of that year. He thought the town was beautiful but poverty widespread: 'I was delighted with Holbeach; a neat little town; a most beautiful church with a spire ... gardens very pretty; fruit trees in abundance ... and land dark in colour and as fine a substance as flour ... and when cut deep into with a spade, precisely as to substance like a piece of hard butter, yet nowhere is the distress greater than here.'[33]

Cobbett found that hogs and fat sheep were better fed and cared for than were labouring people – so many of them refugees from the drainage and enclosure of the common that had formerly surrounded the town. He believed that 'God has given us the best country in the world' but we 'have made this once-paradise what we now behold!'[34]

The Education Act of 1870 which made schooling compulsory, as well as new legal controls over agricultural gangs and reduced competition for work because of the migration to urban areas, did lead to a higher proportion of men being permanently employed on farms in the last decades of the nineteenth century. Other gains, including the availability of allotments and the surprising resurgence of the marsh (a paradox that will be explored in a later chapter), also helped restore a degree of social stability and economic security after the trauma of dispossession.

Access to wild foods also continued to moderate Fennish poverty, especially in the late winter when little paid work was to be had: 'Eel pie, no end of eel pie. Once I had to skin four dozen of them', 83-year-old Gladys Otterspoor recalled in the early 1970s. Sparrows, larks and rabbits were also on the menu, although the valuable 'cock larks' ('they seemed to think in London they were a delicacy') were sold.

In the late nineteenth century and the early decades of the twentieth, the Fennish also became widely used as 'black labour' in the groundbreaking agricultural workers' strikes which disrupted the farms of nearby Norfolk for generations. The big farmers to the east would pay men to be on call, ready to step in whenever required.[35]

Gleaning, which remained women's business, continued to be widely practised. In the early twentieth century, the women of Isleham would still walk miles with their children to collect the grain left after the harvest, carrying bundles home on their heads.[36] It is not surprising that some of the older charitable customs also lived on. On 21 December the widows of the Cambridgeshire fens asked for their 'dole' – which was a gift of food or money.[37]

And for those who were fully destitute, there was still poor relief. Dependency on 'the parish' meant proving you were deserving of help to the respectable community members who controlled the distribution of charity. This could make for personalised care; it could also mean rigorous judgement and the workhouse. Few lamented the system's passing when the welfare state reforms of the 1940s finally rendered the ancient Poor Laws redundant.

CHAPTER 13

The Vilification of the Land and its People

The conquest of the Fens did not only rely on new laws, activist courts and a strong army. Integral to the victory over the Fennish was a propaganda campaign designed to break down support for the commoners among members of Parliament and other prominent citizens.

Elements of the PR campaign vilifying the Fens and the Fennish remained unchanged for centuries. These built on ancient prejudices against wetlands which had mythical foundations – stories abound in folklore of heroes and saints going forth to fight giants and demons lurking in murky waters. Beowulf did battle with monsters which haunted the swamps; St Guthlac took on demons living in the marsh; and King Lear invoked the ugliness of the 'the fen-sucked fogs' to 'infect' the beauty of his daughter.

But during the time when the wetland's riches under-pinned the wealth of its monastic residents, Fenland fecundity had been equally celebrated. It was mainly after the move to drain and enclose the Fens began that the swamp was depicted as a place of deprivation and sickness. In the seventeenth century, enclosure apologists like William Dugdale saw the drainage schemes as a salvation for a forsaken people con-demned to living in 'poor desolate places ... where there is no element good'. Dugdale wrote of the 'cloudy' and 'gross' air that emanated from the 'putrid and muddy' water and 'spongy and boggy earth' that was full of 'loathsome vermin'. Even the normally comforting hearth was 'noisome by the stink of smoaky hassocks'.

Such an 'unwholesome' environment was seen to breed near-savages. Dugdale depicted the Fennish as 'a rude and almost barbarous sort of lazy and beggarly people'. William Camden's *Britannia* described the 'Fen-men, or Fen-dwellers' as 'a kind of people according to the nature of the place where they dwell, rude, uncivil, and envious to all others whom they call Upland-men'. They were as 'rough and uncultivated as the soil itself ... marching about on a sort of stilts like giants'.[1]

One drainage defender wrote that the Fennish might be 'justly called the *Great profanum vulgus* of the fens'. Some of them 'lurk like spiders, and, when they see a chance, sally out, and drive or drown or steal just as suits them, and are the Buccanneers of the country'.[2] The poet George Crabbe described the inhabitants of the Fens as a 'joyless ... wild amphibious race/With sullen wo display'd in every face'.[3]

Attacks on the character of the Fennish became particularly crude during periods of active resistance. In 1635, Lieutenant Hammond suggested the people he was trying to control were 'halfe fish, halfe flesh, for they drinke like fishes and sleep like hogges'. Moreover, the people of Ely 'have but a turfy scent and fenny posture about them, which smell I did not relish at all with any content'. Two centuries later, a judge presiding over prosecutions relating to the Littleport riots of 1816* exclaimed: 'Fenmen, disgusting representations of ignorance and indecency.'[4]

In the post-Reformation enclosures, the writings of drainage apologists became infused with a Calvinistic piety that linked reclamation with reformation, as both the fen and its people were seen to be in need of civilised redemption.[5] The fact that many colonists of enclosed land were reformed Protestants fleeing persecution in their home countries gave a human dimension to this godly narrative.[6] From a Calvinist perspective, it was offensive that 'beggars and idle persons' could obtain the essentials of life from the land without conforming to a disciplined daily work schedule.[7] The drainers argued that 'those that live upon the fennes undreyned live a lazy and

---

* While the catalyst for the harshly repressed protests at Littleport and Ely in May 1816 (which saw the military deployed in strength, five protesters hanged and nine others transported to New South Wales) was the hunger and distress associated with the recession which followed the end of the Napoleonic Wars and the return of demobbed soldiers, the vulnerability of the poor to low wages and high grain prices had been greatly exacerbated by enclosure.

unusefull life to the common wealth exercizinge noe trade nor industry'.[8] The people of the Fens were depicted in the same way as indigenous people defending their homes everywhere – idle beings who had forfeited their moral right to possess their country because they did not farm it as God had ordained.

Free access to nature's bounty was assumed to encourage hunters and gatherers towards paganism and savagery. The Fennish shared the fate of the Gael, Australian Aborigine, Native American and Khoisi – a shift to an ordered and civilised agricultural life was seen to be the necessary foundation to their Christian salvation. Such ideology meant that there could be a peculiar idealism inherent to the imperial project. For some conquerors of the marsh, this was work God had called them to undertake – a mission of human salvation founded on the subjugation of the natural world. Samuel Fortrey wrote of 'floods muzzled ... Luxurious rivers govern'd and reclam'd, Streams curb'd with Dammes like Bridles, taught to obey' so that 'New hands shall learn to work, forget to steal. New legs shall go to church, new knees shall kneel.'[9]

Coercion was justified because native contentment with their lot was an otherwise insurmountable barrier to them becoming fully civilised Christians. William Elstobb described the inhabitants of the Fens as a 'hardy, ignorant sort of people, mostly content with such uncomfortable accommodations as nature afforded them, and no way inclined to enter into any great and considerable attempts for improvements'.

Links between the land and the character of its people were also made by the defenders of the common. Their focus was the natural wealth of the Fens that a privileged few were seeking to appropriate for themselves. In his *History of the University of Cambridge* (1665), Thomas Fuller pointed out that:

> the fens preserved in their present property, afford great plenty and variety of fish and fowl, which here have their seminaries and nurseries; which will be destroyed on draining thereof ... Grant them drained, and ... wealthy men would devour the poorer sort of people. Injurious partage would follow upon the enclosures, and rich men, to make room for themselves, would jostle the poor people out of their commons.[10]

The *Anti-Projector* countered the argument that drainage meant a 'rich Improvement' of land that 'was before of little or no value' through observing that: 'The undertakers have always vilified the Fens, and have mis-informed many Parliament men, that all the Fens is a meer quagmire, and that it is a level hurtfully surrounded, and of little or no value: but those which live in the Fens, and are neighbours to it, know the contrary.' The Fens 'breed infinite number of serviceable horses, mares, and colts ... breed and feed great store of young cattle' as well as 'great flocks of sheep' and quantities of 'Osier [willow], Reed and Sedge' and 'Fens fodder, which feeds our cowes in winter'. 'Cole-seed and Rape', the products of the drained farmland, were, the author argued, 'but Dutch commodities ... trash and trumpery'.[11]

Sensitive visitors to the Fens never fully accepted the denigration of the wetland but nevertheless remained biased by an understanding of human disease that associated ill-health with poisonous vapours in the air. Celia Fiennes assumed that the marsh 'needs must be very unhealthy' but acknowledged that the 'natives say to the Contrary'. She saw the Fennish as 'a slothful people' but admitted that 'their Grounds and Cattle' were taken care of.[12] Daniel Defoe pitied 'the many thousands of families that … had no other breath to draw than what must be mixed with those vapours, and that steam which so universally overspread the country'. However, Defoe could also see that the local people were not the forlorn victims that drainage apologists and medical orthodoxy suggested they should be. He noted that although the Fennish were 'not famed for anything so much as idleness and sloth … what the reason of it is, I know not'. Rather, 'the people … live unconcerned, and as healthy as other folks, except now and then an ague, which they make light of, and there are great numbers of very ancient people among them.'[13]

Ague first became widely discussed during the seventeenth century when the deaths of two kings (James I and Charles II) and one Lord Protector (Oliver Cromwell) were partially blamed on their time in the disease-ridden Fens.[14] It is unlikely to be a coincidence that the emphasis on a sickness supposedly spread by the marsh (*mal-aria* literally means 'bad air') corresponded with the first large-scale drainage attempts. Since it was not known until 1880 that malaria was spread by the mosquito, the so-called 'Fen Parson' argued that it was because a 'damp, unhealthy moisture chills the air' where 'Thick, stinking fogs, and noxious vapours fall', that 'Agues and coughs' were epidemical.[15]

One writer suggested that as late as the 1820s many people were still 'fearful of entering the fens of Cambridgeshire, lest the Marsh Miasma should shorten their lives'. Yet by then the longevity of the local people was also widely remarked on. As R. Parkinson pointed out in *Agriculture of the County of Huntingdon* (1811), although sickness 'destroys many of the inhabitants', this was especially so among 'such as are not natives'. He was far from alone in recognising that the local people built up a significant degree of immunity to malaria.[16]

As the push for parliamentary enclosure accelerated, the language justifying dispossession became ever more closely associated with that of the national interest. While this ideology had been growing in influence since Elizabethan times, it became infused by an Enlightenment-inspired belief in the necessity of imposing order on 'waste' lands and 'primitive' people. Such arguments carried extra weight during the 25 years of near-continuous war with the French between 1790 and 1815.[17]

The ideology of 'improvement' was not just about increasing economic output. Over a century ago, in *The Village Labourer*, J.L. and Barbara Hammond noted that the 'improving' ideology was a multi-faceted attack on the commoner way of life. It was about changing the society as much as the economy.[18] From 1793, the reports of the newly established

General Board of Agriculture, largely written by its articulate and activist secretary, Arthur Young, put the improvers' case succinctly. 'I wish I were king', Young had written in 1784; he would 'order the necessary enclosures, buildings, and expenditures for the establishment of farms on tracts now waste. They (the faithful House of Commons) would be happy in promoting the royal pleasures that had for their end the cultivation, improvement and population of the kingdom; making deserts smile with cultivation – and peopling joyless wastes with the grateful hearts of men.'[19]

Young took a particular interest in the Fens, especially the undrained common marshes of Lincolnshire. For Young, this land provided the definitive proof for his thesis: 'So wild a country nurses up a race of people as wild as the fen, and thus the morals and eternal welfare of numbers are hazarded and ruined for want of an inclosure.' The fact that local resistance involved 'laming, killing, cutting off tails, and wounding a variety of cattle, hogs and sheep' was proof that the Fennish were a 'mischievous race'.[20]

Because enclosure apologists were largely in control of what was recorded and documented, their negative view of the productivity of the wetland and its peoples has been widely reproduced by commentators and historians since. In *The Gazetteer and Directory of the County of Huntingdon* (1854), surviving commoners were described as 'relics' of a 'sordid race' – as wild and unproductive as the commons themselves.[21] Macaulay, in his *History of England*, provided a vivid depiction of the 'vast and desolate fen' as a 'dreary region, covered by vast flights of wild-fowl' and 'a half-savage population'.[22]

Associating drainage with 'progress' was the story told by the victors in the fight for the Fens. But the assumption that enclosure was a necessary precondition for an ultimately beneficial increase in agricultural output has remained widespread to this day. This is surprising, given that there is still little empirical evidence for the claim that enclosure increased economic output.[23] It has been over 60 years since the dogged research of Joan Thirsk conclusively rebutted the propaganda of the drainage apologists that undrained fen was an unproductive waste occupied by an unproductive people.[24] Others like J.M. Neeson have gone further and questioned why higher agricultural output should be the main measure of 'progress' anyway: 'Perhaps having "enough" was unimaginable to men who wrote about crop yields, rents, improvements, productivity, economic growth, always *more*, as it has been incomprehensible to twentieth century historians living in constantly expanding market economies.'[25]

Whether the enclosure process was economically beneficial is a cause for legitimate debate. What is clear is that the fecundity of the undrained Fen, as with the character of the Fennish, was denigrated to serve a particular interest. There is also little doubt that the traditional culture did a much better job of looking after the poor. By the early nineteenth century, even Arthur Young recognised the human costs of 'improvement'. He was told by a commoner in 1804 that enclosure had been 'worse than ten wars. I kept four cows before the parish was inclosed, and now I do not keep so much as a goose.'[*][26] Young came to lobby for a legally regulated allotment of land to every villager but was marginalised from the centres of power once he did so, and the Board of Agriculture would not publish his tour of England in which he described the poverty of enclosed villages.[27]

By the second half of the nineteenth century, a degree of sympathy for a conquered people had entered the chronicles of the Fens. With the land and its people transformed, some recognition of what had been lost could be combined with a consoling emphasis on the inevitability of change. W.H. Wheeler asked: 'What cared the Fenmen for the drowning of their land? Did not the water bring them fish, and the fish attract wildfowl, which they could snare and shoot?' However 'important in a national point of view', Wheeler could concede that drainage 'had no attraction whatever in the eyes of the Slodgers'.[28] As with sensitive observers of the fate of the Australian Aborigines and Native Americans, indigenous resistance was to be expected and the destruction of their way of life regretted, but 'history', 'progress' and 'providence' still required that the lament be expressed within an overarching celebration of conquest.

---

[*] Adam Smith reflected on the disappearance of goose-down and linked it with enclosure in Lincolnshire, observing that the geese themselves supplied the quills to sign their own death warrants!

CHAPTER 14

The End of Whittlesey Mere

By 1840, almost all the large bodies of permanent water in the Fens had been drained. However, the biggest of them all, Whittlesey Mere, remained: a symbol both of what had been lost and of what could still be saved. Though diminished by the draining of the surrounding country, scores of species, as well as hundreds of human beings, still relied on it to survive.

The Mere's resources had proved a life-saver for dispossessed Fennish. Collecting birds, fish, reeds, sedge and peat for home use and for sale gave subsistence and supplementary income to local people. The water was also widely used for recreation, festivals and communal gatherings. The best known of these, the annual Feast of the New Club, which included traditional water festivities on the Mere and dancing on the shore, continued to be held on the second Tuesday in June.

During the nineteenth century, tourism also became increasingly important to the local economy as people travelled

to the Mere from surrounding towns and the rapidly industri-
alising city of Peterborough (central to the nation's expanding
rail network) for skating (also a popular spectator sport that
attracted considerable prize money), sledging, regattas (termed
'water picnics') and fishing. Charles Kingsley described skaters
chasing pike visible beneath the ice until the fish became so
exhausted that the ice could be broken and the prize secured.[1]

The ecology of the lake came under increasing pressure
during the nineteenth century as the subsidence of drained
peatlands reduced the flow of water into it. In 1848 Martin
Mere, just south of Whittlesey Mere, was pumped dry and
the English race of the large copper butterfly, *Lycaena dispar*,
became extinct.

The recreational and economic value of the Mere, as
well as its function as an invaluable natural reservoir for flood
waters, meant that proposals to drain it attracted wide opposition. There were also doubts as to whether even the new
steam engines were up to the task. The result was that the
Duke of Bedford's 1830 plan to complete the work of his
ancestors was never carried into effect, and a revised scheme
a decade later shared the same fate.

But in 1851, William Wells of Holmewood returned
home to the Fens after visiting the celebration of British
technological and territorial expansion known as the Great
Exhibition. Among the more than 100,000 items on display
at London's purpose-built Crystal Place were the latest inno-
vations in steam technology. Britain's transformation into the
first industrial nation was being built on steam power and the

Exhibition proudly displayed the mighty new engines being developed in the factories that were becoming the workshops of the world.

At the Great Exhibition, Wells had seen the newly invented Appold's Centrifugal Pump. Capable of pumping 1,600 gallons of water per minute, this pump was considerably more effective than the earlier generation of steam engines that still relied on scoop wheels. Wells persuaded his wealthy neighbours, John Heathcote of Conington Castle, Edward Fellowes of Ramsey Abbey, George Thornhill of Diddington Hall, Lord Sandwich, and Wentworth Fitzwilliam of Milton to jointly finance and undertake, in conjunction with the Middle Level Commissioners, the drainage of Whittlesey Mere.[2]

That it was already well known that subsidence from peat loss would inevitably follow the drainage is evidenced by the fact that Wells had a twelve-foot cast iron column (reputedly taken from the dismantled Crystal Palace) driven into ground level at Holme Fen adjacent to the Mere. The exposure of the column was intended to provide a measure of subsequent soil loss.

Thousands of local people and visitors witnessed the drainage of the Mere, which the new pumps achieved with speed and efficiency. Thousands of fish and eels were collected as the waters receded. Also exposed in the mud was a glorious fourteenth-century censer (a ceremonial incense burner) used in masses at Ramsey Abbey, now considered the finest European example of its time. Had it been hidden in the lake at the time of the dissolution? Other items seen in the bed of the vanquished Mere included a chandelier, a boat, the skull of a wolf and the skeleton of a killer whale.

While the drainage of the Mere was presented as proof of Britain's scientific and technological achievements, the same increase in applied knowledge made it more difficult to claim that the drainage was of national economic benefit. The inevitable subsidence in land meant a heavy expense in repairs of buildings and even railways.[3] The private windfall was obvious but the degree to which this equated with the public interest was disputed. However, the idea that a government or even non-government body might intervene to save the natural environment was still decades away from being seriously imagined.

Mid-Victorian faith in the innate virtue of progress was still evident in the destruction of the Mere. This idealism was particularly visible in the activities of the Duke of Bedford, who owned 18,500 acres around Whittlesey and by 1875 had spent about £200,000 remaking his drained estate, including constructing a new Thorney village to a design by S.S. Teulon.[4]

The ploughing of the Mere bed seemed to signal the final conquest of the Fens and the indigenous culture that depended on it. But the pumps had to be restarted after a flood in 1852 refilled the lake, and again in 1862 when a sluice gave way and the waters returned for a last time. The reason that this was to be the final resurrection for Whittlesey Mere was that, unlike the surrounding marsh, the silt and sand bottom did not shrink when exposed to the air, meaning that the former bed was soon higher than the peatlands surrounding it. By 1875, the iron column sunk by Wells already stood over eight feet high.

The Mere was drained just before the introduction of photography could provide a permanent record of what had been lost. But Charles Kingsley, who visited the site of the lost lake in 1877, gave a vivid picture of the transformation that had occurred:

> [W]hat a grand place, even twenty years ago, was that Holme and Whittlesea, which is now but a black unsightly steaming flat, from which the meres and the reed-beds of the old world are gone ... grand enough it was, that black ugly place, when backed by Caistor Hanglands and Holme Wood and the patches of primeval forest; while dark green alders, and pale green reeds, stretched for miles round the broad lagoon, where the coot clanked, and the bittern boomed, and the sedge-bird, not content with its own sweet song, mocked the notes of all the birds around; while high overhead hung motionless, hawk beyond hawk, buzzard beyond buzzard, kite beyond kite, as far as an eye could see ... They are all gone now. No longer do the ruffs trample the sedge into a hard floor in their fighting rings, while the sober reeves stand round, admiring the tournament of their lovers ... Gone are ruffs and reeves, spoonbills, bitterns, avocets; the very snipe, one hears, disdains to breed. Gone too, not only from the Fens, but from the whole world, is that most exquisite of butterflies – *Lycaena dispar* – the great copper; and many a curious insect more.[5]

In his lament for a vanished world, Kingsley was also anticipating the new. Nostalgia for vanished beauty would be the driving force behind environmental activism in late Victorian England. Most people now lived in cities far removed from nature and the old way of life, and the commons-depleted villages were also changing fast. The sense of loss associated with the diminished connections to community, customs and nature would drive a new-found concern with conserving the countryside.

If Whittlesey Mere had been drained a generation later, it is likely to have had its share of painters, poets and conservationists to proclaim its beauty and call for its preservation.* But even the late nineteenth-century imagination was culturally constrained when it came to imagining possibilities for change. Progress might be critiqued, and the loss of old ways regretted, but this lament was still generally expressed within a dominant narrative of the inevitability of the process underway. By peculiar paradox, it was not to be those who wrote eulogies for the beauty of lost landscapes that would save the scattered marshes still surviving in the Fens, but the hard-headed free-market economic reformers whose triumphant ideology was creating the modern world.

* One of the most significant figures in nature conservation in Britain, Charles Rothschild (1877–1923), bought part of Wicken Fen in 1899 and donated it to the National Trust, who manage it to this day. In 1910, he purchased Woodwalton Fen and donated this to an organisation he founded, the Society for the Promotion of Nature Reserves – now known as the Royal Society of Wildlife Trusts.

CHAPTER 15

An Incomplete Victory: The Enclosed Fens to 1939

With the draining of Whittlesey Mere it seemed that the fight for the Fens was over. The small areas of remnant marsh were being rapidly reclaimed by the resurgent steam engine whose power seemed to have no limits. Why then did the area of wetland actually expand in the Fens between 1870 and 1939?

To understand this paradox, it is first necessary to consider the fundamental one underpinning it: the more efficient any drainage scheme in the Fens was, the more it increased the problem to be solved. The main reason for this is that peat decomposes when exposed to air, which meant drained land got lower over time. Further peat loss from compression, the erosion of bare soil (which came to be called 'fen blow'), the removal of soil on root crops, and the deliberate and accidental burning of dry peat exacerbated subsidence. Because the wetlands were only marginally higher than sea level in the first place, their drainage was always a work in progress, requiring ever-stronger pumps just to maintain the status quo. As land succumbed, not only did the movement of water slow down but higher levels of sediment were deposited, further inhibiting the release of water to the sea. Fenland rivers, which had never found an easy path into the strongly tidal and sediment-heavy Wash, needed continual dredging to keep flowing at all. Moreover, as water courses sat ever higher above the adjacent land, the pressure on their artificial banks grew and floods became more likely when they broke.[1] In 1813, W. Gooch observed that most of the fen banks were made of 'fen-moor and other light materials', meaning that 'a great part of the water soaks back again' and under sufficient pressure, banks could burst altogether.[2] The end result was that every improvement in technology increased the drainage challenge for the next generation.

The forces of nature worked against the gravity-dependent Dutch drainage schemes from the start. In 1695, Celia Fiennes had recorded that in the supposedly drained Great Level, the 'ffens are full of water and mudd'; the causeway to Ely was flooded, and the inhabitants 'have no way but boates to pass in'.[3] And in 1713, the Denver sluice, the key to Vermuyden's system, was washed out to sea. A partial solution was provided through employing windmills. Large wooden wheels were fitted with paddles or ladles which scooped water a few feet at a time out of lower drains to higher ones.[4] Windmill efficacy was assisted by developments in under drainage, with clay pipes put below the surface to get water out of the fields. However, windmills were not only expensive to construct but labour-intensive to operate (one benefit being that many dispossessed Fennish got relatively autonomous work maintaining and running them).[5]

It was the limits of wind technology that ensured the partial protection of 'drained' fenland for centuries after enclosure. Some areas were allowed to return to marsh to act as a reservoir to hold winter waters and were only used for summer grazing. In the early nineteenth century, Arthur Young found that much former agricultural country had returned to 'sedge and rushes, frogs and bitterns!'. The largest example of this was the 20,000 acres between Wisbech and Downham Market, which was in 'so wild a state' that its only product was 'sedge and turf'.[6]

During the eighteenth century, large areas of drained land also had to be periodically flooded to allow the restoration of the soil. Peat, made from rotting plant matter, builds up quickly when vegetation is flooded, so a rotation system came to be widely employed in the Fens. By the end of the century, it was common for only a third of a farm to be cultivated at once, with the rest seasonally inundated. Drained land was farmed for four to six years before it became too low for windmills to keep dry, at which point the water was returned until the peat was sufficiently restored for the pumps to do their work.[7] This form of land use provided a refuge for diverse wetland species and facilitated Fennish hunting and fishing, giving space for people to adapt and survive.

The system of land management meant that in 1800, while the enclosed country was very different from the medieval fen, it was still more akin to it than the modern one. Moreover, the drained regions were becoming wetter, not drier. Even the most generous rotation did not allow peat to build up as quickly as it decomposed, meaning that the long-term trend was for a decline in the quantity of agricultural land. Diminishing returns meant that the region was in turn less attractive to investors whose capital was needed for any large-scale drainage scheme. Young suggested in the early nineteenth century that with 'two or three more floods ... 300,000 acres of the richest land in Great Britain will revert to their ancient occupiers, the frogs, coots, and wild ducks of the region'. He believed that 'the Fens are now in a moment of balancing their fate; should a great flood happen within two or three years, for want of an improved outfall, the whole country, fertile as it naturally is, will be abandoned'.[8]

The reason that nature did not triumph in the nineteenth century was solely because of the power of steam. The new drainage era that opened in 1819–20 with the installation of a steam pump near Littleport seemed to offer a permanent solution to an intractable problem. The technology developed so fast that within 50 years the force that drove the Industrial Revolution seemed to have finally achieved the sustainable drainage of the Fens. The invention of a machine to cheaply manufacture the pipes laid underneath tilled country sealed the engineer's apparent victory.[9] While not even the full force of the Industrial Revolution could change the contradiction inherent to fen drainage – the more water extracted, the faster the land subsides – the consequences of this were overcome by employing ever more powerful pumps: steam, diesel and ultimately electric.

A problem delayed is not, however, a problem solved. This truth was revealed when agricultural prices collapsed in the 1870s, making the economics of ever more intensive drainage an increasingly marginal proposition.

The price of grain fell because of the low cost of production in North America and the availability of cheap steam-powered transport to bring it to market. While growing demand meant that the impact of the mid-Victorian abolition of the 'Corn Laws' (which had imposed a tariff on imports) had not been immediately apparent, by the turn of the century New World grain was replacing the home-grown commodity. The area of cultivated land in England declined from 1893 until the start of the Second World War as pasture expanded and the area of 'waste' land increased.[10]

The collapse in agricultural prices meant that the most ambitious scheme for fen drainage ever conceived was not fulfilled. An Act of Parliament was obtained for draining much of the Wash to create 150,000 acres of land to be called the Victoria Level, but cheap American imports ensured that the scheme was put on permanent hold. Indeed, no further significant marsh reclamation at all was undertaken after 1875 as big investors looked abroad for more profitable agricultural investments.[11]

A further benefit of the agricultural recession for the survival of Fennish culture came from the fact that the cheap imported food did not threaten smallholders. While grains could be transported cheaply from abroad, this was not true of most vegetables and fruit, which still needed to be grown closer to the point of consumption. The fertile soils of the Fens enabled small farmers to quickly switch production from grain and find a profitable niche selling a broad range of produce to urban consumers benefiting from cheap bread and higher wages. The ability of smallholders to change crops every season according to market demand meant that even farms of five acres or less could be viable. As late as 1937, 55 per cent of holdings in the Holland district were fewer than twenty acres in size.[12] Rich soil, a mild climate and a skilled and entrepreneurial smallholder tradition meant that, almost uniquely in England, the token acreages conferred to commoners on enclosure could potentially provide economic independence. With the undrained or partially drained country still rich in fish, game, reeds and fuel, thousands of Fennish farmers were able to support their families, supplement incomes and sustain community life.

Such was the resilience of the Fennish that they became the object of national attention for reformers lamenting the decline of farming. As Joan Thirsk has concluded, 'By the close of the nineteenth century, agricultural writers dwelt less upon the misfortunes of the smallholder than upon his resilience. It was agreed that he of all the farmers of Lincolnshire had suffered least' from the importing of cheap food.[13] In the early twentieth century, H. Rider Haggard reported that the Isle of Axholme 'is one of the few places in England which may be called truly prosperous'.[14]

During the late nineteenth century, the idea of the common was also revived. In 1887, Thomas Scrutton, Professor of Constitutional Law at Kings College London, was awarded the Yorke Prize by the University of Cambridge for his research on *The History and Policy of the Laws Relating to Commons and Enclosures in England*. Scrutton's thesis was that 'The ownership of the legal rights of an individual over land stand on a different footing from any other class of property', because while 'landlords may own' land, 'the English people have to live on it'. Mainstream liberal thought increasingly agreed with Scrutton that it was essential to 'keep the land of England from becoming closed to the people of England'.[15] For the first time in over 200 years, part of the political class sought to protect what was left of the common.

The Commons, Footpaths and Open-Spaces Preservation Society, founded in 1865, was a leader in the movement that led to a series of laws passed to protect 'open space' (including the 74 commons of former villages within fifteen miles of the centre of London that became parklands) and to maintain footpaths and access to the countryside.[16] One organisation that grew out of this concern for conservation, the National Trust, purchased over 600 acres of Wicken Fen in 1899. This reserve was so well studied by academics from nearby Cambridge University that it became critical to the development of ecology as a science.[17]

The priority of late nineteenth-century commons defenders was the preservation of open space and natural beauty rather than the commoners' way of life. But there was some concern for the traditional small farmers, and gains for the dispossessed in improving public access to the countryside.

The granting of small allotments of land to the poor also became increasingly common after the General Enclosure Act of 1845, with enclosures through legislation ceasing altogether in 1870 (although 'voluntary' enclosure continued).[18] Related action was also taken to increase access to already enclosed land. Local authorities purchased about 1,600 acres of the former Holland Fen between 1887 and 1894 to divide into one-acre allotments to be let to labourers. In addition, a benevolent aristocrat, Lord Carrington, released 658 acres to be divided into allotments of one to four acres among 200 tenants. New societies and cooperatives were formed, including the Spalding Cooperative Small Holdings Society and the South Lincolnshire Small Holdings Association. These bodies rented more land from the enlightened Lord to sublet, started a co-op bank, and sought to purchase equipment and sell produce on a collective basis.[19]

These concessions pointed to the fact that at the local level the *memory* of loss remained a potent force for change. Marx believed that 'memory of the connexion between the agricultural labourer and the communal property had ... vanished' during the nineteenth century, but the evidence suggests otherwise.[20] Chippenham commoners reclaimed their

fen common near Soham in the 1830s, more than a generation after parliamentary enclosure and 200 years after their
ancestors had first resisted drainage.[21] In the Isle of Axholme,
awareness of history played a major part in the protection of
the remaining open fields. Well into the twentieth century, the
prevalence of poaching in the Fens rested on the recollection
of the greater theft that created the crime.

E.P. Thompson documented how through the nineteenth
century, 'the ground-swell of rural grievance came back always
to access to the *land*'.[22] J.M. Neeson has shown how 'the sense
of loss, the sense of *robbery*' that persisted 'as the bitter inheritance of the rural poor' continued to be captured in village
poetry including the many manifestations of the widely cited
ditty: 'The fault is great in man or woman,/Who steals a goose
from off a common;/But what can plead that man's excuse,/
Who steals a common from a goose?'[23]

The power of memory was also probably evident in the
imperial settler's longing for land. The millions of descendants
of dispossessed commoners who chose lives of hardship in the
back blocks of the United States, Canada, Australia and New
Zealand suggests a need that cannot be explained by rational
self-interest alone. Even the freed convicts of Van Diemen's
Land, so many of them urban folk with no direct experience
of farming or hunting, 'went bush' in the notorious island col-
ony to find freedom from imperial magistrates and masters.[24]
As the dispossessed became dispossessors, the tragic intergenerational impacts of English enclosure stretched around
the globe.

Twentieth-century technology brought new pressures on the Fens environment and Fennish culture. As the impact of industrialisation spread into the remotest regions of England, the value of some of the products of the marsh declined, which in turn influenced land management. E.A.R. Ennion recalled that in his region of Cambridgeshire, 'up to 1900 the fen had been yielding its natural resources, turf, litter and reeds to generations of local villagers', with simple sluices still used to 'control' the water rather than 'banish it'. Through their management of the wetland, the villagers had preserved the peat as a sustainable energy source. However, the adoption of coal-fired iron stoves and fireplaces, combined with the move from thatch to slate roofing, meant that by 1910 'the demand for natural products had almost ceased', and fires 'which hadn't been out for years' in open hearths went cold, 'the reedbeds stood unwanted in the fen' and 'no one cut the sedge'.[25] But Ennion documents that 'nature started to reassert herself' when agricultural prices once again collapsed in the early 1920s, and 'held unbridled sway' until the renewed demand created by the Second World War.[26]

The survival of Fennish culture was also facilitated by the ongoing isolation of much of the region. Away from the railway, the drained land was nearly as remote as the old fen. Holbeach in Lincolnshire became the largest parish in England after its surrounding marsh was drained, with some people living twelve miles from their parish church. In the Cambridgeshire fen village of Isleham, many folk had never been to Cambridge, let alone London or the sea; and 'strangers' stood out until car travel revolutionised transport in post-war decades.[27] Institutions of state and big business could be equally distant and, in this void, the Fennish were able to maintain their own cultural traditions.

One measure of this is that in 1851 there were 831 non-conformist chapels in Lincolnshire, more than the total number of parish churches, and the highest concentration of these were in the Fens.[28] The Baptist, Primitive Methodist, Congregational and other chapels were managed and ministered to by local people without wealthy patrons, state support or endowment, and only scant contact with the central administration. The religious revival associated with the re-churching of the Fens was also critical to the rebuilding of communities in the decades following enclosure; with the empowered lay leadership representing community interests to employers and state institutions and developing new forms of mutual aid.

Ennion remembered that his community was mainly made up of 'Stout Nonconformists all, who wouldn't do a stitch beyond feeding their animals' on the Sabbath, yet 'they nevertheless caught fish on Sundays'.[29] Babies could be taken to be 'churched' or blessed, but not necessarily baptised. Some of the vigour of religious life can also be sensed 'from the vast corpus of hymns they have left behind them – the unexplored, unrecognised folk-poetry of England'.[30]

Another measure of the strength of local identity was the continued reluctance of the Fennish to fight in England's wars. In 1803 the Defence of the Realm returns highlighted that even at the height of the fear of an imminent French invasion, the Fens were not providing many recruits to the armed forces. National mobilisation had little success in the region until 1914, and even then 'the queues of recruits seen in other parts of the country did not materialise'.[31] People undoubtedly saw themselves as English, but the meaning that flowed from this identity coexisted with a deeper belonging associated with home.

The vitality of the Fennish was also evident in their continuing cultural evolution. The most publicised innovation of the nineteenth century was in the sport of skating. The first skates were square wooden boards or platters used when wildfowling, but a long shallow blade was developed by local skaters in the 1800s. Fennish skaters became renowned for their speed, skill and distinct style – easily recognisable because they held both hands behind their backs. But as many old people of the Fens recall, skating was also done for fun. The popularity of recreational skating (and indeed swimming) was facilitated in the pre-war years because so much water still remained. It is also true, though, that 'we don't get winters like we did then'.[32]

Hunting techniques, in addition, continued to adapt. The old eel traps made of willow were supplemented in the 1800s with nets. Birds could be killed with high-tech mounted guns as well as shot traps and decoys. Hunting ceased in 1947 because of conservation concerns, although it was the destruction of habitat that was the primary threat to the avian population.

In 1873, Charles Kingsley had regretted the loss of the birds of Whittlesey Mere: 'They are all gone now … Ah, well, at least we shall have wheat and mutton instead, and no more typhus and ague; and, it is to be hoped, no more brandy-drinking and opium-eating; and children will live and not die.'[33] But what Kingsley could not know, and as a man who took for granted the inevitability of progress would never have believed, was that the destruction he documented had then reached its nineteenth-century apogee.

Despite the technology and political power of the drainers, and the seeming never-ending march of the modern world, on the eve of Second Word War, more of the wetland survived than it had in 1870. Continued access to undrained coun- try meant that many Fennish had been able to endure the onslaught of the Industrial Revolution, adapt to the opportun- ities of the market economy and preserve significant elements of their culture. Such had been the resilience of the people and the land that few could have predicted how quickly the demands of total war would remake the Fenland and transform the old way of life that had survived with it.

CHAPTER 16

Dry For Ever?
The Fens in the Post-War World

In his 1942 memoir, *Adventurers Fen*, E.A.R. Ennion described the destruction of his homeland that was then occurring as a result of the wartime food emergency:

> It is more than a year since the red and white surveyor's poles glinted above the reeds, blazing a trail for the draglines that were soon to follow ... In a few short weeks the scoops had torn a channel twenty feet wide from end to end, ripping the backbone out of Adventurers Fen. The water from the ditches and the interlines, the moisture from the peat, bled in an endless trickle into the deep new drain ... When all was dry men set the fen on fire ... Reed beds, sedges and sallows vanished in a whirl of flying ashes amid the crackle and the roar. I went down afterwards. There was a single gull wheeling over the dead black land and a wild duck trying

to hide in two inches of water at the bottom of a drain. A couple of tractors stood waiting to begin. There is dignity in standing corn, a graciousness in the wide drills of potato fields starred with gold-spiked lilac bloom. But I regret the sacrifice of those glorious bird-haunted wastes of reed and water for the growing of sugar beet. No crop is less in sympathy with an English landscape than this alien ... But beet means ... sugar produced at home.

Also lost was a bittern's nest, the first that had been recorded 'in the county for close on a hundred years'.[1]

Adventurers' Fen lies just south of the neighbouring and much studied Wicken Fen, which had been drying out and losing its birdlife due to the drainage of surrounding land. By contrast, Adventurers' Fen was full of wildfowl until it was destroyed.

Ennion, no less a patriot than the Ministry of Agriculture men who organised his fen's destruction, was conscious that the drainage was the latest expression of the priority long given to the products of farmland: 'It was the old, old cry: is not a fat sheep better than a goose, a stalled ox better than a dish of eels?'[2]

In 1944, the owner of the farm that encompassed Adventurers' Fen, Alan Bloom, published his own book, *The Farm in the Fen*, seemingly in response to Ennion's lament. Bloom had purchased his property in the early 1930s and just like the enclosure apologists of earlier centuries, vigorously defended the economic and social benefits of drainage.

Bloom worried that Britain had lost interest in agriculture and become complacently reliant on food imports. The dangers of this had been revealed by the German U-boat blockade and the author hoped that those who read his book 'may become conscious of a conviction that land, good land, now that it has been so hardly won back from dereliction, should never again be neglected or diverted from its true purpose'.[3]

Ennion and Bloom were documenting the final chapter in the centuries-long struggle between those who had sustained a way of life connected to the fen, and people who sought to privatise and drain it in partnership with the state. But in their competing narratives can also be seen the beginning of the post-war contest between a new type of environmental consciousness and an affirmation of the primacy of continual economic development.

In this struggle of ideas and interests, the drainers emerged triumphant. Any chance that the wartime drainage would be a temporary phenomenon was ended by the challenges posed by post-war austerity, a new commitment to an expanded role for the state, and the need to respond to the devastating floods of 1947 and 1953. After over 300 people died in the latter inundation, massive government-funded projects were implemented to guarantee the safety of the region.[4]

The costs of these projects were never intended to be commensurate with the agricultural output of the perman-ently drained land. However, this calculation changed after Britain's entry into the European Economic Community, when farmers began to receive heavily subsidised prices for their products. Investment in fen farms rapidly increased in the 1970s and 1980s, ensuring that even the tiny patches of marsh that had survived the big engineering schemes were made dry.

The end-result of the post-war drainage effort, by far the most capital-intensive in the history of the Fens, is that over 99.9 per cent of the original wetlands have now been drained.[5] The landscape was as comprehensively transformed between 1950 and 2000 as at any corresponding period in history.

But in this millennium, there are signs that the permanently dry landscape might prove to be as provisional as those that preceded it.

Despite the rapid advances in technological capacity and scientific knowledge, the contradiction inherent in all fen drainage schemes – the more successful the solution to the drainage problem, the greater the problem becomes – has remained intractable. The success with which the land has been kept dry in the past 60 years has only accelerated peat loss and subsidence. The fertility of the soil and thus the profitability of the farms are being reduced just as the cost of pumping water increases due to rising energy prices. It is now not uncommon for a field to be six or ten feet below the rivers flowing between the ever-higher floodbanks above it. Reduced agricultural subsidies (whose very existence is uncertain as Britain departs the European Union) and a central government less willing to engage in public infrastructure spending, means that keeping the entire region dry will not be sustainable over the long term. The likelihood that some farmland will return to marsh is increased by the fact that the population of many districts has dropped due to capital-intensive farming and the rise in car ownership.

There are also significant uncertainties around climate change. Even under conservative forecasting scenarios, sea level rise is likely to lead to the seasonal or permanent inundation of much of the Fens without the construction of sea walls of prohibitive size and expense. Ironically, another long-term problem posed by a changing climate is a shortage of fresh water for farm, business and household use. Uncertainty will impact on investment choices and farmers' ability to raise capital to deal with the rising waters. Ultimately there can be little doubt that global heating is likely to lead to large areas of currently farmed country returning to wetland.

The fact that around 90 per cent of South Holland is now below sea level and that even areas around Ely, 30 miles from the coast, have sunk lower than the sea, makes a change in land management unavoidable.[6] This is not, however, unusual in historical terms. In Roman times, the sea level was 23 feet lower than it is today. The sea rose from about AD 375 and then again in the thirteenth century when yet another new coastline formed. Likewise, the rivers have always changed course – the old routes, or 'roddons', can still be seen from the air because of their sandy beds.

Because the current spate of environmental change is occurring at the same time as heightened environmental awareness, it is not surprising that many people are actively imagining a different future for the Fens. Hard-headed economists, rational planners, concerned land managers and farmers have joined with conservationists and passionate local people to restore wetland and recreate traditional land management. The future being worked out in reserves and flood management zones, such as Welney Wetland Centre, the Ouse Washes, Wicken Fen and Hatfield Moors, involves managing the environment through periodic inundation, seasonal grazing (that creates the right grass height for many breeding and wintering birds), and cutting of sedges and reeds. The goal of the new conservation is what the Fennish achieved for centuries – living *with* the waters rather than fighting them. In the Fens, even the most ardent nature-lover understands that the country has always been a *human*-managed landscape. Restoring the natural wealth of the Fens does not mean ending farming but actively managing the land through applying scientific and traditional knowledge.

The most significant attempt at cultural and natural restoration is the Great Fen Project. In an area of about fourteen square miles encompassing and surrounding the old Whittlesey Mere, a number of groups are collaboratively working to restore the vanished fen. Different landscapes are being created – wet meadow, reedbeds, open water, dry meadow, and woodland. Although it is not possible to restore the Mere itself because of the subsidence of the peatland surrounding it, other areas of open water and marsh will connect fragmented existing reserves, such as Woodwalton Fen and Holme Fen, to facilitate a functioning ecosystem.[7]

The necessity of the Great Fen Project can be seen at the Holme Fen National Nature Reserve that abuts the vanished

Whittlesey Mere. One hundred and seventy years of peat loss means that the lowest point in the UK is now in this reserve – nine feet below sea level. The twelve-foot column hammered into ground level in 1851 had been completely revealed by the 1950s, so that a new post needed to be erected next to it to document the ongoing subsidence. More than twenty feet of soil has now disappeared.

Much of Holme Fen is now woodland, but the resilience of nature is seen in the fact that over 70 species of birds are again breeding in the Great Fen area (even the bittern is now a regular visitor) and some vanished species of butterflies have returned, as well as the ruddy darter dragonfly. The fen woodrush, a plant found nowhere else in the British Isles, has survived, as have over 500 fungi. Long-dormant seed is sprouting into plants not seen in generations (one farmer of the old Mere bed, John Bliss, reflected in 1986 that when you dig bog oaks out, 'You get all sorts of weed seeds out from six feet down … all sorts of things that you don't see nowadays. Some quite strange.').[8]

Despite all the signs of natural and cultural resilience, loss *is* loss. The Great Fen Project will not be able to replicate the full glory of the former wetland. Not even the most sophisticated scientific breakthrough will bring back the swallowtail butterfly or the full diversity of other species that used to live in the region. Nor can the rich culture and localised land management practices of the Fennish be reproduced through knowledge garnered from fragments of memory, photos, writings, records and archaeological digs.

But what indigenous peoples across former imperial realms have shown is that confronting loss can be a foundation for sustaining a continuing connection to country based on the wisdom of ancestors, scientific knowledge *and* the needs of the modern age. The campaigners, villagers, farmers, and urban dwellers who are working to reimagine land management for the twenty-first-century fen, are heirs of centuries of struggle to protect the land and its people.

Restoration, reclamation, natural forces and climate change are almost certain to lead to increased areas of wetland in the twenty-first century. But what does this mean for the common? Is it possible that this traditional way of relating to the land might also be revived?

The Royal Commission that investigated the common lands of England and Wales in the 1950s documented their almost complete disappearance in the Fens. A region that formerly had one of the highest areas of common land now had one of the lowest. The loss of some commons had been surprisingly recent. In Isleham Washes, 376 acres of common land had been purchased and enclosed by the Ministry of Agriculture in 1947, leaving just small village greens, 45 acres of grazing ground and heightened poverty for poor villagers.[9] Wicken Poor's Fen was an area set aside at enclosure, where sedge was cut and peat dug up by commoners until the First World War. Significant areas of Cambridge itself of course remained open – protected by perhaps the most powerful common defenders in the nation.[10]

The village of Soham benefited from its relatively late

enclosure. But still only 5 per cent of the original common remained open, with four 'poor's commons' totalling 158 acres for general use and three 'horse' fens of 110 acres intended for horses who ploughed the open fields. There was also an unregulated 'Broad Piece' and 400 acres of charity land (to provide an income for the parish to support those who lost all means of subsistence at enclosure).[11]

Lincolnshire was even worse off than Cambridgeshire. There was almost no common land left in the entire county. Holland, where the Fennish had successfully resisted enclosure for so long, made a 'nil return' of common land to the Royal Commission.[12]

The only significant exception in the county was the Isle of Axholme. The commissioners noted that 'the villages of Belton, Epworth and Haxey were given rights of turbary over large areas'.* There were seven turbaries – the designated peat-harvesting zones – in all, comprising 524 acres. Although the right to cut peat was no 'longer exercised except over some very small areas' and most of the land had become scrub, even in the 1950s the common was performing one of its traditional functions – providing a refuge for travellers and 'squatters'. One 20-acre common at Waddingham was 'unused except by gipsies' ponies'. Fifty acres in Belton Big Turbary had been 'converted into good pasture with grazing controlled by a Farmers' Committee'. Both Epworth Turbary and the

---

* Turbary was the common right to collect peat, or as it was called in the Fens, 'turf', for fuel.

150-acre Haxey Turbary had already been designated as Sites of Special Scientific Interest and remain reserves to this day.[13]

The commissioners noted that there were many small areas of common land where the 'historical evidence shows that in the Inclosure awards some allotments were made ... for the poor of the parish' and for other uses, but for 'the most part they cannot even be traced today'. The commissioners dourly concluded that 'most would simply seem to have been quietly annexed by neighbouring owners'.[14]

Most remarkable was the survival of unenclosed open fields still cultivated in strips by local farmers with customary rights. The fact that Epworth and Haxey are among the very few places in England where they can still be seen is not a historical accident but a testament to the success of nearly four centuries of resistance. Their existence is proof that the men and women who were injured, imprisoned, exiled and even gave their lives in the long struggle to keep possession of their ancestral homeland were not forgotten in the Isle. Generation after generation of villagers believed that it was their duty to do what their ancestors had done for them – defend and pass on to their children their just inheritance. All the fragments of common land which remain in Axholme are important not just for heritage, conservation and recreational purposes but for the story of struggle they convey.

In the twenty-first century, there is a renewed interest not just in saving what is left of the old common but in creating new ones. As recently as 1968, the ecologist Garrett Hardin assumed that a commons would inevitably be over-exploited because it is in the interest of each commoner to access its resources to the maximum extent that they are able. Since it is 'rational' to increase personal wealth without regard to the wider community, how could a common resource not be plundered?[15]

The problem with the 'tragedy of the commons' hypothesis is that the history of the Fens (and countless other commons) shows it to have been a well-managed country that provided sustainable resources for thousands of years. In 1700, the Fens was not the depleted, over-hunted, over-fished, over-grazed environment that Hardin's theory suggested it should be. This was because use of resources was embedded in communal relationships that did not merely police how people behaved but guided how they lived. The Fens were sustainably managed because the Fennish were *not* just motivated by their own material gain. Hardin was wrong about the commons because he was wrong about the commoners.

The commons are being reimagined across the globe as part of the fightback against liberal economic theory's reductionist perspective on human beings. Are we *only* self-serving consumers or are we also inherently relational, seeking forms of belonging with each other and the natural world? History provides evidence for both postulations but the fact that most people in most places have lived in common, suggests that free-market economic theorists got human nature fundamentally wrong. Since the global financial crisis, even many economists seem to agree. Elinor Ostrom's receipt of the Nobel Prize for her extensive work on the commons reflected the fact that this subject is no longer only of interest for historians, anthropologists or alternative lifestylers.[16] It will surprise no one who has studied the history of the Fens or other commonly managed societies, that the 'tragedy of the commons' is no longer a serious thesis. Human beings are motivated by many factors, but people have *always* engaged in self-sacrifice to defend their home from those who would destroy it. The global environmental challenge of the twenty-first century is not, at least in this sense, any different from that faced by the Fennish for millennia – how best to resist, adapt, accommodate and survive?

The Post-Imperial Fen

Where are we going, then? Homewards, always.
Novalis (translated from the German by Tom Webber)

It is an irony of history that during the same period that the Puritans departed from Boston seeking freedom from religious persecution, other Protestants *arrived* in the Fens port with the same purpose in mind. Both groups of God-fearing settlers colonised the lands of an indigenous people whose perspective on country could not have been more different from their own. For the newcomers, the land needed to be redeemed by being tilled; for the native, the country was part of who they were – not a place needing salvation but one that conferred it.

If the centuries of Fennish resistance to enclosure, drainage and colonisation had occurred anywhere but England there would be no dispute that this was another example of an indigenous people resisting the appropriation and destruction of their homeland.

The fact that the Fennish shared the same nationality as the colonisers of the New World (indeed after their own dispossession, they sometimes joined their ranks) has determined how their story has been told. But how much did being 'English' change the Fennish experience? Was a commoner's perception of what was happening to them primarily determined by nationality? What consolation was citizenship to a person being dispossessed from the only home they knew?

The Fennish story is an integral part of the troubled history of the imperial age. As elsewhere in the empire, an indigenous people fought the land grab through every means available to them, including force, until the subversive power of the modern state and the technological power of the Industrial Revolution achieved what seemed to be a final victory.

That the Fennish also used the courts and lobbied Parliament in their long campaign, accommodated the invader as well as confronting them, adapted to *and* resisted the newcomers, and rarely adopted a single strategy or spoke with one voice, is true not just of their fight but of almost every other arena of indigenous struggle. Resistance is always a complex multi-faceted process, not a Western movie.

The suffering consequent to conquest required providential justification in the old Boston as much as the new. Across the empire, colonisers' founding narratives provided assurance that the fate of dispossessed native peoples was not their fault. Concepts of divine providence, the benign energy of free enterprise, the inevitability of progress, the unstoppable power of technology and the unfolding of social evolution crossed the seas. The providential mythology of the United States is better promoted but something similar is also, if more modestly, to be found in narratives of the drainage and enclosure of the Fens.

In the mid-eighteenth century, W. Pennington recognised the imperial similarities. In *Reflections on the Various Advantages Resulting from the Draining, Inclosing and Allotting of Large Commons and Common Fields* (1769), he argued that although the inhabitants of the Boston fens would be hurt by enclosure, it made as much sense to preserve the commons as to evacuate North America: 'Let the poor native Indians … enjoy all their ancient privileges, and cultivate their own country their own way. For 'tis equal pity, notwithstanding some trifling dissimilarity of circumstances, that they should be disturbed.'[1] Pennington had a point. To defend the rights of the Fennish to keep possession of their lands would have undermined the ethical legitimacy of empire. As an anonymous defender of the commons put it in 1780, to justify enclosure, the proponent must 'bring himself to believe an absurdity before he can induce himself to do a cruelty'.[2] That absurdity was the idea that appropriating another's homeland could be a benign act which ultimately benefited the dispossessed.

Justification for the suffering inflicted on the poor through drainage and enclosure could also be callous and crude. While English nationality and a white skin provided the Fennish with a level of protection from racism, the safety this afforded during periods of active resistance should not be exaggerated. In such circumstances, the people were depicted as savages – as useless as the country they defended. R.H. Tawney observed that the enclosers 'depicted the fens as a swamp, useful only then, through drainage ... and their inhabitants as a population sub-human in its lawlessness, poverty and squalor. Piety and profits demanded, it was felt, the reclamation of both.' Seventy years ago, when Tawney wrote these words, it was still obvious that this was 'the attitude of the white settler to the agricultural crudities and social irregularities of an African tribe'.[3]

That the dispossessed sometimes became the dispossessor does not change the injustice of enclosure but highlights its implications across generations. As an investor in the Virginia Company, Robert Gray, observed, when the 'commons of our Country lay free and open for the poore Common[er]s to injoy ... we had not great need to follow strange reports, or to seeke wild adventures, for seeing we had not onely sufficiencie, but an overflowing measure proportioned to everie man'.[4]

The conquest of the Fens and the dispossession of the Fennish was therefore not a precursor to the imperial story but part of it. And as in other regions of the empire, there was nothing inevitable about the conquest of the Fens. Choices were made.

Recognition of this fact is important because how the past is understood frames how we imagine the future. When history is seen to be determined by forces beyond human control (be it God, the free market, 'manifest destiny' or 'progress'), what point is there in seeking change? Otherwise vastly different Marxist, conventional-progress and popular-global histories are often ahistorical in the sense that they reduce people to pawns in an unfolding drama with a predetermined end. Such narratives can also fall prey to technology-worship – as if possession of the capacity to drain explains the decision to drain.

Indigenous people can be pitied in determinist history, but their resistance is inherently futile. The disempowering impact of such historiography has been highlighted since dispossessed people began actively documenting their survival story. There have now been decades of research revealing how conquered peoples were not passive victims but active agents in resisting the tumult and tragedy that befell them. And it is not only the conquered peoples of former colonies who need to know that their ancestors' defence of their homeland ensured that all was not lost.

The drainage and enclosure of the Fens took hundreds of years to complete (if that is the right word for the provisional dryness achieved). The main reason that the process took so long was the success of the resistance. The Fennish of south Lincolnshire and the Isle of Axholme prevented the draining of their country for over a hundred years. What was so futile about that? Karl Polanyi in *The Great Transformation* rightly asked: 'Why should the ultimate victory of a trend be taken as a proof of the ineffectiveness of the efforts to slow down its progress?' Polyani knew that the 'rate of change' is as important as the change itself. Indigenous cultures conquered in decades have a very different history than those conquered over centuries because time gives the ability to adjust and adapt.[5]

The old Fens *is* now a lost landscape. The amnesia this fostered has allowed culturally ingrained prejudices against unproductive, untamed and unhealthy swamps to continue to exist. But while the wondrous Fennish wetland has largely been forgotten, the ache for what has been lost has never entirely disappeared. In the nineteenth century one observer recalled:

> We, perhaps, confess, that things are better as they are; yet we cannot dissemble our regret at the change. Gladly we would recall the water fowl that have taken their flight from these regions, never to return ... Again as we picture to ourselves the lovely insects, which, after swarming for ages amid the willows and water plants of Lincolnshire, have become lost, not only to the county but to England, within the memory of living man; or when in some rich herbarium we examine the faded specimens of aquatic plants, whose place in the British Isles knows them now no more, how can we help longing to look out upon the scene that met the eye of Asgeir, Askr, and Hundolf ... It may be mere sentiment, yet it is sentiment springing from the loving sympathy that knits one generation to another, and forms a bond between man and the world of nature that ministers to his wants.[6]

The irony is that the Fens, the part of England's countryside that has been most comprehensively destroyed, is also the region that might now be most quickly restored.

The Fens have always been a country on the move, existing as both a natural landscape and a human-created one, changing from century to century, year to year, and season to

season because of environmental change and human intervention. Impermanence is integral to the spirit of a land created
by the flow and fluidity of water. All that has ever been geographically fixed is a few islands, the sky and a vast horizon
– an unchanging reference point for the shifting waters below.
Rising seas and sinking soils do require changes in land management, but in this part of England there is nothing new
about that.

ACKNOWLEDGEMENTS

In recent years, whenever people conversationally asked me 'What book are you working on now?', and I explained that I was doing a book on the resistance to the drainage of the Fens, I knew the next question would be 'Why?' This response is understandable given that I live in Tasmania and am best known as a historian of colonial Australia (who has sometimes branched out, but never quite so far). It is a question that deserves an answer.

I lived in Britain a number of times from my late teens through to my early thirties (including having the good sense of marrying an Englishwoman). In one of those periods I was a social worker with the aged people's team at Norfolk County Council, based in Norwich. While our office didn't cover the county's portion of the Fens to our west, my 'patch' did extend into the Norfolk Broads. A joy of my job was meeting old farm hands. While we filled in the endless forms required to receive a service from a modern bureaucracy, I heard their stories about life on the land. I am grateful to these elders and the friends and colleagues who helped me connect with the Norfolk earth. It was from there that I first journeyed into the homeland of my own ancestors. My mother's family, the Peets, lived for many centuries in the Lincolnshire fen village of Horbling (Great Uncle Henry Peet was one of the local historians); while the Boyces have been farmers of the Cambridgeshire fens for generations. I don't know if I am related to James Boyce, a leader of the resistance to drainage and enclosure in the mid-seventeenth century, but I like the fact that it is a real possibility! While this direct ancestral connection was not consciously part of the origin of this book, it has added interest, depth and mystery to the labour of writing it. And we are still discovering how many memories are carried in our genes.

A more direct source for this book was my research on the Australian frontier. Here, with the guidance of many fine historians, I came to learn what a complex place it was. Once the tragic reality of invasion and conquest is faced up to honestly, the multifarious forms that resistance can take, including accommodation and adaptation, can be explored.

When I began to read histories of the Fens, I was struck by some largely unacknowledged similarities with the colonial frontier. Here too was a multi-faceted defence of country, a transformation of the land, the introduction of foreign settlers and a confrontation between two worlds. While researching *Australian* history, I began to wonder, did the fact that the Fens was a part of *England* justify such a radically different approach to writing its past?

The massive step from 'question' (the beginning of all history) to book-writing only came after I felt the relationship to the Fens that more gifted writers than me have explained so well (none better than Graham Swift in *Waterland*). The

ACKNOWLEDGEMENTS

Fens might be nearly all drained now but when you walk on this contested earth, you don't just feel the ache of what has been lost but the wonder of what is still there (contrasting emotions I know well from the troubled history of my own island home). Sleeping by the vanquished Whittlesey Mere, once the largest lake in lowland England, under the vastness of the Fens sky, I felt the wonder of the relationship between humans and nature on which any environmental history relies.

Once a decision to spend years writing a new book is taken, for an independent historian the debts soon accumulate. I thank the Australia Council for the Arts, Arts Tasmania and the University of Tasmania, whose under-valued library staff helped garner the documents I needed to proceed. In our cluttered and over-stimulated world, keeping the book alive has become one of the great cultural resistance stories. One day a historian will try and explain this achievement, and will highlight the commitment, passion and depth of the people engaged in the industry. In this instance, Anna Carmichael and Ben Fowler at Abner Stein, and Tom Webber and Andrew Furlow at Icon Books ensured that a lifeless Word document could be transformed into the living book that Ruth Killick and Nadia Manuelli helped launch into the world. I am particularly grateful for the skill, care and local knowledge that Duncan Heath brought to editing the manuscript.

Equally essential to the writing of *Imperial Mud* was family backing. I thank my wife Emma, my children, Clare and William, and my parents, sisters and friends for supporting me to enjoy a privileged but sometimes marginal writing career.

My English friends and family, June Pattinson, Mary Bingham, Bill Bingham, Susie McAlpine, Matt Bingham, Jim Bingham and their extended clans, make England feel like home.

I also want to acknowledge some people I have never met, but whose scholarship is the foundation of this book. All history is built on the work of others, but I was particularly struck, in the research for this one, what a monumental labour (sometimes over a lifetime) was undertaken by a small number of scholars: H.C. Darby, Joan Thirsk, Keith Lindley, Ian Rotherham, Francis Pryor and Eric Ash notable among them. I was particularly fortunate that two highly relevant doctoral theses, by Betty Brammer and Heather Falvey, have been completed in the past decade. Both deserve a wider audience.

Finally, my thanks are owed to the magnificent people of the Great Fen Project. This passionate team are working to restore a functioning ecology in the area around the old Whittlesey Mere. Walking back to my car after a few days unauthorised camping (being an old-fashioned historian, I still need to sleep on it before I can write about it), I was met by the land manager and a policeman. I stood ready to make a fulsome apology, but none was needed. Just as they cared for the land, they were caring about me; worried about what had become of an Australian who had left a hire car in the middle of nowhere.

I am grateful for not having been arrested. I am even more thankful for subsequently being given a tour through the Great Fen and shown the wonderful environmental and cultural restoration work which is showcasing a new way to make home in the wetland. Care for people, care for country; surely it is that on which the future of not just the Fens, but of our world, now depends.

NOTES

A note on describing the Fens and the Fennish

1. D.J. Stewart, ed., *Liber Eliensis*, 1848, 4; cited in Dorothy Summers, *The Great Level: A History of Drainage and Land Reclamation in the Fens*, David and Charles, Newton Abbot, Devon, 1976, 30–1.

Foreword

1. There are exceptions to this narrative of progress in Fens historiography. The most notable in recent years has been Ian D. Rotherham's *The Lost Fens: England's Greatest Ecological Disaster*, The History Press, Stroud, 2013.

Chapter 1

1. James C. Scott has argued that 'Sedentism and the first appearance of towns were typically seen to be the effect of irrigation and of states. It turns out both that both are, instead, usually the product of wetland abundance.' James C. Scott, *Against the Grain: A Deep History of the Earliest States*, Yale University Press, New Haven and London, 2017, xi.

2. James C. Scott critiqued the 'nearly indelible association of civilization with the major grains' and observed that 'within this perspective, swamps, marshes, fens and wetlands generally

have been seen as the mirror image of civilization – as a zone of untamed nature, a trackless waste, dangerous to health and safety.' James C. Scott, *Against the Grain*, 55.

3. James C. Scott, *Against the Grain*, 68.

4. *Beowulf, A Verse Translation* by Michael Alexander, Penguin Books, Harmondsworth, Middlesex, 1973, 54.

5. This quote is from the interpretation panel at English Heritage's Flag Fen Prehistoric Fenland Centre where the boats are on display. For a fuller description of the history and archaeology of the Flag Fen site, including its discovery and excavation, see Francis Pryor, *The Fens: Discovering England's Ancient Depths*, Head of Zeus, London, 2019.

6. Francis Pryor, *English Heritage Book of Flag Fen Prehistoric Fenland Centre*, B.T. Batsford, London, 1991, 120–21.

7. Because of the smell of rotting fish and its tendency to attract flies, remains were likely to be disposed of in water or some distance from camp. Fish bones are also small and do not survive well, especially in acid soils. Francis Pryor, *English Heritage Book of Flag Fen Prehistoric Fenland Centre*, B.T. Batsford, London 1991, 130.

8. H.E. Hallam, *The New Lands of Elloe: A Study of Early Reclamation in Lincolnshire*, Department of English Local History Occasional Papers No. 6, University College of Leicester, 1954, 3.

9. H. Petrie and J. Sharpe, eds, *Monumenta Historica Brittanica*, 1848; Jeremy Purseglove, *Taming the Flood: A History and Natural History of Rivers and Wetlands*, Oxford University Press, 1988, 35; Dorothy Summers, *The Great Level: A History of Drainage and Land Reclamation in the Fens*, David and Charles, Newton Abbot, Devon, 1976, 11.

10. Stephen Rippon, *The Transformation of Coastal Wetlands: Exploitation and Management of Marshland Landscapes in North West Europe during the Roman and Medieval Periods*, Oxford University Press, 2000, 127–8.

11. Garrick Fincham, *Landscapes of Imperialism: Roman and Native Interaction in the East Anglian Fenland*, Archeopress, Oxford, 2002, 7–8.

12. Fincham further suggests the interruption of the ceramic sequence might represent an explicit rejection of the Roman way of life. Garrick Fincham, *Landscapes of Imperialism*, 16, 83.

13. Stephen Rippon, *The Transformation of Coastal Wetlands*, 69–71; Jeremy Purseglove, *Taming the Flood*, 40.

14. Ian D. Rotherham, *The Lost Fens*, 28.

15. Christopher Marlowe, *Legends of the Fenland People*, E.P. Publishing, Wakefield, 1976 (first published Cecil Palmer, 1926), 3–6.

16. *Ibid.*, 7–17.

Chapter 2

1. A programme of archaeological survey and excavations from the late 1970s to the mid-1990s revealed the extent of early medieval settlement of the fenland. Before that, the accepted view was essentially that of monastic chroniclers – that after the Roman withdrawal the Fens had returned to wilderness. Stephen Rippon, *The Transformation of Coastal Wetlands*, 169.

2. Felix, *Life of St Guthlac*, 1848 edition, 21.

3. H.E. Hallam noted in 1954 that 'the constant references to the wilderness seems odd when a stream of visitors come to see the saint'. His servants included 'Beccel the priest, his constant

friend and confidant, and Wilfrith … one of Felix's authorities' for the biography. H.E. Hallam, *The New Lands of Elloe: A Study of Early Reclamation in Lincolnshire*, Department of English Local History Occasional Papers No. 6, University College of Leicester, 1954, 6.

4. Valerie Gerrard, *The Story of the Fens*, Robert Hale, London, 2003, 61.

5. H.E. Hallam, *The New Lands of Elloe*, 3.

6. There are local stories of monks being friends of the people, but equally stories of monks who oppressed them, and the need to protect vulnerable local women from their unwanted attention. Maureen James, *Cambridgeshire Folk Tales*, The History Press, Stroud, 2014, 62–3.

7. Francis Pryor, *English Heritage Book of Flag Fen Prehistoric Fenland Centre*, B.T. Batsford, London, 1991, 10.

8. Maureen James, *Cambridgeshire Folk Tales*, 62–3.

Chapter 3

1. Neil Walker and Thomas Craddock, *History of Wisbech and the Fens*, 1849.

2. Derek Wall, *The Commons in History: Culture, Conflict and Ecology*, The MIT Press, Cambridge, Massachusetts, 2014, 7, 25–26.

3. Writing in the 1880s, W.H. Wheeler argued that 'although to a great extent, the Fenland had been parcelled out in grants to the followers of the Conqueror, the Normans were never able to subdue the Fenmen to the same state of vassalage as the inhabitants of other parts of the country. Instead of the Fenmen becoming Normans in manner and language, the Normans

gradually became converted into Fenmen.' He observed that 'in the ordinary conversation of a Lincolnshire Fenman in the present day is to be found purer Saxon English than in any other part of the country. It was from the fen town of Bourne that "the poet and patriarch of true English", Robert Manning of Brunne, as he was generally called, went (A.D. 1300) to Cambridge, where he became "the first great writer in modern classic English."' W.H. Wheeler, *The History of the Fens of South Lincolnshire*, second edition, 1888 (first published 1868), 30.

4. D.C. Douglas, *Feudal Documents from the Abbey of Bury St Edmunds*, 1932, cxxxii; William Page, 'The Middle Level of the Fens and its Reclamation', in Granville Proby and S. Inskip Ladds, eds, *A History of the County of Huntingdon*, Volume 3, 1936, 249–90.

5. Stephen Rippon, *The Transformation of Coastal Wetlands*, 250–1.

6. Nicola Whyte, *Inhabiting the Landscape: Place, Custom and Memory, 1500–1800*, Windgather Press, Oxford, 2009, 26.

7. David Roffe sees the 1189 fight as 'symptomatic of more widespread changes in a society' away from customary communal associations to formal manorial ones. He believes that 'the bounds of Crowland as expressed by the five rivers that surround the island' represented 'some sort of ancient territory'. In other words, the Fennish were fighting for the right to retain full access to their traditional lands. H.E. Hallam, *The New Lands of Elloe*, 30–1; Derek Wall, *The Commons in History*, 71–2.

8. Katharine Sykes, *Gilbertine Lecture*, Spring Wells Heritage Group, April 2009, 5–7, 12–13, 16–17.

9. Dorothy Summers, *The Great Level*, 34; Oliver Rackham, *The History of the Countryside*, Weidenfeld & Nicolson, London, 1993 (first published 1986), 387.

10. W.H. Wheeler, *The History of the Fens of South Lincolnshire*, second edition, 1888 (first published 1868), 34.

11. Stephen Rippon, *The Transformation of Coastal Wetlands*, 223–5.

12. William Page, 'The Middle Level of the Fens and its Reclamation', in Granville Proby and S. Inskip Ladds eds, *A History of the County of Huntingdon*, Volume 3, 1936, 249–90.

13. *Ibid.*, 249–90.

14. Valerie Gerrard, *The Story of the Fens*, Robert Hale, London, 2003, 72.

15. Joan Thirsk, 'Fenland Farming in the Sixteenth Century', Department of English Local History Occasional Papers No. 3, University College of Leicester, 1953, 42–5.

16. Dorothy Summers, *The Great Level*, 35, 43.

17. William Page, 'The Middle Level of the Fens and its Reclamation', 249–90.

18. Eric H. Ash, *The Draining of the Fens*, Johns Hopkins University Press, Baltimore, 2017, 69–70.

19. Stephen Rippon, *The Transformation of Coastal Wetlands*, 209.

20. Dorothy Summers, *The Great Level*, 40–1.

21. Stephen Rippon, *The Transformation of Coastal Wetlands*, 208.

22. *Ibid.*, 252–3.

23. Stephen Rippon, *The Transformation of Coastal Wetlands*, 175.

24. W.H. Wheeler, *The History of the Fens of South Lincolnshire*, 30.

25. *Ibid.*, 38.

Chapter 4

1. Peter Linebaugh, *The Magna Carta Manifesto: Liberties and Commons for All*, University of California Press, 2008, 48–9.

2. Thomas Edward Scrutton, *Commons and Common Fields or The History and Policy of the Laws Relating to Commons and Enclosures in England*, Cambridge University Press, 1887, 75–6.

3. *Ibid.*, 74–5.

4. Peter Linebaugh and Marcus Rediker, *The Many-Headed Hydra: Sailors, Slaves, Commoners, and the Hidden History of the Revolutionary Atlantic*, Beacon Press, Boston, 2000, 17–18.

5. Peter Linebaugh, *The Magna Carta Manifesto*, 53–4.

6. Between 1545 and 1600 the population of England and Wales increased by about 45 per cent, from under 3 million to over 4 million people. By 1650, the population had reached about 5.25 million. This increase was associated with a land short-age in some regions, the reclamation of wastes and woodlands, the migration of people in search of work and land, higher prices for agricultural products, a prolonged decline in real wages for the labouring poor and a shift to market production. David Underdown, *Revel, Riot and Rebellion: Popular Politics and Culture in England 1603–1660*, Oxford University Press, 1987, 18.

7. Keith Lindley, *Fenland Riots and the English Revolution*, Heinemann Educational Books, London, 1982, 8.

8. Joan Thirsk, 'Fenland Farming in the Sixteenth Century', Department of English Local History Occasional Papers No. 3, University College of Leicester, 1953, 34–5.

9. Joan Thirsk, *English Peasant Farming: The Agrarian History of Lincolnshire from Tudor to Recent Times*, Routledge and Kegan Paul, London, 1957, 38.

10. Joan Thirsk, 'Fenland Farming in the Sixteenth Century', 24–5.

11. As Joan Thirsk has pointed out, the increase in stock numbers alone is 'incompatible with any theory of widespread and continuous inundation'. *Ibid.*, 25.

12. *Ibid.*, 31–3.

13. *Ibid.*, 41–2.

14. Jeremy Purseglove, *Taming the Flood*, 31–2.

15. Betty Brammer, *The Holland Fen: Social and Topographical Changes in a Fenland Environment, 1750–1945*, PhD Thesis, Centre for English Local History, University of Leicester, 2009, 47–8.

16. H.C. Darby, *The Draining of the Fens*, Cambridge University Press, 1940, 9–10.

17. Ian D. Rotherham, *The Lost Fens*, 51–2.

18. H.C. Darby, *The Draining of the Fens*, 10.

19. Maureen James, *Cambridgeshire Folk Tales*, 7.

20. 'Tewing' means 'to haul, tow (a ship, net, etc.), to drag, pull, tug'. Carr is 'a fen or bog' possibly 'grown up with low bushes, willows, alders, etc.'. Stover is 'winter food for cattle'. H.C. Darby, *The Draining of the Fens*, Cambridge University Press, 1940, 26–7.

21. Eric. H. Ash, *The Draining of the Fens*, 62–5.

22. Humphrey Bradley, *Treatise*, 1589, in Dorothy Summers, *The Great Level*, 8.

23. Eric H. Ash, *The Draining of the Fens*, 150–68.

24. H.C. Darby, 'The Draining of the Fens A.D. 1600–1800', in H.C. Darby, ed., *An Historical Geography of England before 1800*, Cambridge University Press, 1936, 444; Jeremy Purseglove, *Taming the Flood*, 46.

25. H.C. Darby, 'The Draining of the Fens A.D. 1600–1800', 444.

26. H.C. Darby, *The Draining of the Fens*, Cambridge University Press, 1940, 50.

27. Eric H. Ash, *The Draining of the Fens*, 172.

28. Keith Lindley, *Fenland Riots and the English Revolution*, Heinemann Educational Books, London, 1982, 33–5.

29. *Ibid.*, 36–8.

30. *Ibid.*, 40.

31. *Ibid.*, 40–1.

32. H.C. Darby, *The Draining of the Fens*, 50–1.

33. William Camden, *Britannia, or a Chorographical Description of the Most Flourishing Kingdomes, England, Scotland, and Ireland …*, translated by Philémon Holland, London, 1610, 491. Emphasis original.

34. Eric H. Ash, *The Draining of the Fens*, 302–6.

35. H.C. Darby, *The Draining of the Fens*, Cambridge University Press, 1940, 38–9.

36. H.C. Darby, 'The Draining of the Fens A.D. 1600–1800', in H.C. Darby, ed., *An Historical Geography of England before 1800*, Cambridge University Press, 1936, 448.

37. David Blackbourn, *The Conquest of Nature: Water, Landscape and the Making of Modern Germany*, Pimlico, London, 2007, 28.

38. H.C. Darby, *The Draining of the Fens*, 40.

Chapter 5

1. A powte was a lamprey, which is an eel-like fish. The ditty was reproduced In Dugdale's 1662 *History of Imbanking and Drayning of Diverse Fennes and Marshes*, and cited in Jeremy Purseglove, *Taming the Flood*, 52.

2. Jeremy Purseglove, *Taming the Flood*, 49.

3. G. Stovin, *The History of the Drainage of the Great Level of Hatfield Chase in the Counties of York, Lincoln and Nottingham*, 1761.

4. Keith Lindley, *Fenland Riots and the English Revolution*, Heinemann Educational Books, London, 1982, 83–6.

5. *Ibid.*, 96–7.

6. *Ibid.*, 92.

7. H.C. Darby, *The Draining of the Fens*, 56.

8. H.C. Darby, *The Draining of the Fens*, 56; Keith Lindley, *Fenland Riots and the English Revolution*, 98–100.

9. Keith Lindley, *Fenland Riots and the English Revolution*, 97.

10. H.C. Darby, *The Draining of the Fens*, 61.

11. Keith Lindley, *Fenland Riots and the English Revolution*, 100–01.

12. *Ibid.*, 101–2.

13. H.C. Darby, *The Draining of the Fens*, 102.

14. Keith Lindley, *Fenland Riots and the English Revolution*, 102–4.

15. *Ibid.*, 101.

16. Jeremy Purseglove, *Taming the Flood*, 59–60.

17. Keith Lindley, *Fenland Riots and the English Revolution*, 105–9; Christopher Hill, *God's Englishman: Oliver Cromwell and the English Revolution*, Weidenfeld & Nicolson, London, 1970, 49.

Chapter 6

1. Maurice Ashley, *The Greatness of Oliver Cromwell*, London, Hodder and Stoughton, 1957, 25–7; Christopher Hill, *God's Englishman: Oliver Cromwell and the English Revolution*, Weidenfeld & Nicolson, London, 1970, 46.

2. H.C. Darby, *The Draining of the Fens*, 55–6; Jeremy Purseglove, *Taming the Flood*, 52.

3. W. Dugdale, *A Short View of the Late Troubles in England*, 1681, 460; Christopher Hill, *God's Englishman: Oliver Cromwell and the English Revolution*, 49.

4. The Long Parliament's grievance was that large 'quantities of common and several grounds hath been taken from the subject by color of the Statute of Improvement, and by abuse of the commission of sewers, without their consent and against it'. Eric H. Ash, *The Draining of the Fens*, 436.

5. Keith Lindley, *Fenland Riots and the English Revolution*, 117–19.

6. *Ibid.*, 143.

7. *Ibid.*, 168–9.

8. *Ibid.*, 170.

9. Peter Linebaugh, *The Magna Carta Manifesto: Liberties and Commons for All*, University of California Press, 2008, 83–4.

10. Eric H. Ash, *The Draining of the Fen*, 481.

11. *Ibid.*, 552–64.

12. Keith Lindley, *Fenland Riots and the English Revolution*, 170.

13. Dugdale recorded that in 1657 'there were no less than 11,000 men sometimes imployed at work, at a time'. Sir William Dugdale's Diary, 1657, 'Things observable in our Itinerarie begun from London 19 May 1657', reproduced in H.C. Darby, *The Draining of the Fens*, Appendix III, 273.

14. Keith Lindley, *Fenland Riots and the English Revolution*, 173–5.

15. *Ibid.*, 176–7.

16. *Ibid.*, 177.

17. Jeremy Purseglove, *Taming the Flood*, 52.

18. Keith Lindley, *Fenland Riots and the English Revolution*, 176–9.

19. H.C. Darby, *The Draining of the Fens*, 76–7.

20. Keith Lindley, *Fenland Riots and the English Revolution*, 182.

21. *Ibid.*, 183.

22. '*An Ordinance for the Preservation of the Works of the Great Level of the Fenns*, Ordered by his Highness the Lord Protector, and His Council, That this Ordinance be Forwith Printed and Published, Fryday May 26, 1654', London, 1654.

23. Keith Lindley, *Fenland Riots and the English Revolution*, 183–4.

24. *An Ordinance for the Preservation of the Works of the Great Level of the Fenns*, London, 1654.

25. Keith Lindley, *Fenland Riots and the English Revolution*, 186.

26. Anon. (John Maynard?), *The Anti-Projector: Or The History of the Fen Project*, 1653?.

27. Christopher Hill, *'The World Turned Upside Down': Radical ideas during the English Revolution*, Temple Smith, London, 1972, 291.

28. Keith Lindley, *Fenland Riots and the English Revolution*, 230–1.

29. *Ibid.*, 230–1.

Chapter 7

1. Paul Middleton, *England's Lost Lake: The Story of Whittlesea Mere*, Fast Print Publishing, Peterborough, 2018, 4.

2. Heather Falvey, *Custom, Resistance and Politics: Local Experiences of Improvement in Early Modern England*, PhD Thesis, University of Warwick, Department of History, 2007, 296.

3. The petitioners included James Boyce, Ralph Boyce, John Colls, Robert Dowe, William Dowe, Ralph Easeom, William Freeman, Isaac Gardner, John Henson, Adam Kelfull and Richard Searle. Heather Falvey, *Custom, Resistance and Politics*, 299; Keith Lindley, *Fenland Riots and the English Revolution*, 116.

4. Heather Falvey, *Custom, Resistance and Politics*, 303–4.

5. Andy Wood, *Riot, Rebellion and Popular Politics in Early Modern England*, Palgrave Macmillan, Basingstoke, 2002, 103; Heather Falvey, *Custom, Resistance and Politics*, 305.

6. Heather Falvey, *Custom, Resistance and Politics*, 308.

7. Heather Falvey, *Custom, Resistance and Politics*, 307, 363–4. See also Henry Peet, ed., *Register of Baptisms of the French Protestant Refugees settled at Thorney, Cambridgeshire, 1654–1727*, Huguenot Society, Aberdeen, 1903.

8. Heather Falvey, *Custom, Resistance and Politics*, 308; Keith Lindley, *Fenland Riots and the English Revolution*, 144. The continuity of the Walloon community is recorded in Henry Peet, ed., *Register of Baptisms of the French Protestant Refugees settled at Thorney, Cambridgeshire.*

9. The quotation comes from the 1643 petition of the Earls of Bedford and Portland against the rioters. Cited by Heather Falvey, *Custom, Resistance and Politics*, 310–11.

10. Keith Lindley, *Fenland Riots and the English Revolution*, 158–9; Heather Falvey, *Custom, Resistance and Politics*, 310–11.

11. Heather Falvey, *Custom, Resistance and Politics*, 312.

12. *Ibid.*, 313–16.

13. Keith Lindley, *Fenland Riots and the English Revolution*, 5–6; C. Holmes, 'Drainers and Fenmen: the Problem of Popular Political Consciousness in the Seventeenth Century'; in A. Fletcher and J. Stevenson eds, *Order and Disorder in the Seventeenth Century*, Cambridge University Press, 1985, 179, 182–3; Heather Falvey, *Custom, Resistance and Politics*, 317–22, 327.

14. Heather Falvey, *Custom, Resistance and Politics*, 322, 329–30.

15. *Ibid.*, 336–41.

16. *Ibid.*, 347–8.

17. Letter from Colonel Valentine Walton, 21 June 1648, to the Committee at Derby House, cited in Heather Falvey, *Custom, Resistance and Politics*, 349.

18. Heather Falvey, *Custom, Resistance and Politics*, 356.

19. *Ibid.*, 359–61.

20. Celia Fiennes, *Through England on a Side Saddle in the time of William and Mary being the Diary of Celia Fiennes*, The Leadenhall Press, London, 1888.

21. CRO: 1261M91, Manuscript volume of copies of 'Decrees and other Documents Transcribed from a Book made from the [Whittlesey] Town Copies and examined therewith this

18th Day of July 1821', compiled by John Boyce, cited in Heather Falvey, *Custom, Resistance and Politics*, 365.

Chapter 8

1. W.G. Hoskins and L. Dudley Stamp, *The Common Lands of England and Wales*, Collins, London, 1963, 22–3.

2. William Read, *Read's History of the Isle of Axholme: From the Earliest Period until the Act of Enclosure of the Commons in 1795*, Epworth, Read and Co., 1858, facsimile edition, Epworth Mechanics' Institute, 1980, 30.

3. Hatfield Chase had reverted to the Crown in 1347 and forest law applied. It was perhaps the largest deer park in England. Ian D. Rotherham, *The Lost Fens: England's Greatest Ecological Disaster*, The History Press, Stroud, 2013, 64–5.

4. William Read, *Read's History of the Isle of Axholme*, 52–6.

5. In 1657, the ruins of the old manor of the Lords of Mowbray 'on the south side of the Churchyard' could still be glimpsed in a cornfield, according to Sir William Dugdale, 'Things observable in our Itinerarie begun from London 19 May 1657', reproduced in H.C. Darby, *The Draining of the Fens*, 281.

6. Keith Lindley, *Fenland Riots and the English Revolution*, 26–7.

7. Arthur Young, *General View of the Agriculture of Lincolnshire*, David and Charles, Newton Abbot, Devon, 1970 (first published 1813), 19–20.

8. Joan Thirsk, 'The Isle of Axholme before Vermuyden', *Agricultural History Review* 1, cited in Jeremy Purseglove, *Taming the Flood*, 29.

9. Keith Lindley, *Fenland Riots and the English Revolution*, 27.

10. *Ibid.*, 72–4.

11. *Ibid.*, 75–6.

12. *Ibid.*, 77.

13. Because of the troubles in the Isle, some settlers soon moved south to the Great Level, where the Earl of Bedford welcomed them by restoring the disused church of Thorney Abbey for their use. Jean Tsushima, 'Melting into the Landscape: The Story of the 17th-century Walloons in the Fens', in Randolph Vigne and Charles Littleton, eds, *From Strangers to Citizens: The Integration of Immigrant Communities in Britain, Ireland and Colonial America, 1550–1750*, Sussex Academic Press, Brighton, 2001, 108–12.

14. Keith Lindley, *Fenland Riots and the English Revolution*, 19–20.

15. *Ibid.*, 30–1, 78.

16. *Ibid.*, 30–1.

17. *Ibid.*, 65–7.

18. *Ibid.*, 149.

19. *Ibid.*, 152.

20. 1,000 acres each was to be given to Lilburne and Wildman, and 200 acres to Noddel in return for their assistance. Keith Lindley, *Fenland Riots and the English Revolution*, 199, 208. See also Eric H. Ash, *The Draining of the Fens*, 473–5.

21. Keith Lindley, *Fenland Riots and the English Revolution*, 198–9.

22. *Ibid.*, 199.

23. *Ibid.*, 212.

24. The General found that in October 1650 Epworth and Belton residents had put their cattle into the settlers' corn and left them there until the following June. From 11 June 1651 to the end

of that month, they also pulled down 84 dwellings belonging to the settlers, as well as other buildings (including a windmill). Whalley confirmed that a 'very great Ryot was committed at Sandtoft in the said Isle on 19 October, being the Lords Day in the year 1651', in which 'Lieut Colonel John Lilburn and Mr Noddel coming thither, who placed two men with their swords by their sides at the Church door, the said Lieutenant Colonel Lilburn saying that … they came to take possession of the Church and that the Minister should not preach there, nor the people hear… [and] that on the 21st of January 1655, diverse of the Inhabitants of the Isle, purll'd down and break in pieces, the windows, dorrs, seates and Pulpit of that Church, and that some of those men discharged two Gunnes'. The broken pieces of the doors, windows, pulpit, etc. were laid in the middle of the church and set on fire.

25. When Dugdale came through Sandtoft in 1657, the chapel was still in a 'very ruinous' condition. Sir William Dugdale, Diary 1657, 'Things observable in our Itinerarie begun from London 19 May 1657', Appendix III in H.C. Darby, *The Draining of the Fens*, 281.

26. Keith Lindley, *Fenland Riots and the English Revolution*, 222, 233–4.

27. *Ibid.*, 237; Eric H. Ash, *The Draining of the Fens*, 462.

28. Keith Lindley, *Fenland Riots and the English Revolution*, 241–2.

29. *Ibid.*, 246–9.

30. *Ibid.*, 250–1.

31. Ralph Waller, *John Wesley: A Personal Portrait*, SPCK, London 2003, 7.

32. *Ibid.*, 10.

33. W.B. Stonehouse, *The History and Topography of the Isle of Axholme*, London, Longman, Rees, Orme and Co., 1839, 165. The likely connection between the burning and commoner protest has often been missed, perhaps because it did not fit well with Methodist folklore. H.N. Brailsford was a prominent exception, observing that: 'The feud of these turbulent peasants against the landed gentry was still raging in the next generation, when they burned down Epworth parsonage and the child John Wesley had to be snatched from the flames.' H.N. Brailsford, *The Levellers and the English Revolution*, Spokesmen Books, 1976, 610.

34. There is a further note by Young dated 1808: 'The enclosure has taken place, and answered to an extraordinary degree'; Arthur Young, *General View of the Agriculture of Lincolnshire*, David and Charles, Newton Abbot, Devon, 1970 (first published 1813), 57, 100–01.

35. W.B. Stonehouse, *The History and Topography of the Isle of Axholme*, xii–xiii.

36. *Ibid.*, 12, 33.

Chapter 9

1. Betty Brammer, *The Holland Fen: Social and Topographical Changes in a Fenland Environment, 1750–1945*; PhD Thesis, Centre for English Local History, University of Leicester, 2009, 47–8.

2. Keith Lindley, *Fenland Riots and the English Revolution*, 54–5.

3. *Ibid.*, 47–9, 55–6.

4. Dorothy Summers, *The Great Level: A History of Drainage and Land Reclamation in the Fens*, David and Charles, Newton Abbot, Devon, 1976, 106.

5. Keith Lindley, *Fenland Riots and the English Revolution*, 54.

6. H.C. Darby, *The Draining of the Fens*, 62.

7. Keith Lindley, *Fenland Riots and the English Revolution*, 114–15.

8. *Ibid.*, 119–20.

9. *Ibid.*, 122–3.

10. *Ibid.*, 124.

11. *Ibid.*, 125–32.

12. *Ibid.*

13. Keith Lindley, *Fenland Riots and the English Revolution*, 135–6.

14. *Ibid.*, 145.

15. *Ibid.*, 223–4.

16. Joan Thirsk, 'Seventeenth-Century Agriculture and Social Change' in Joan Thirsk, ed., *Land, Church and People: Essays Presented to Professor H.P.R. Finberg*, British Agricultural History Society, 1970, 173.

17. Daniel Defoe, *A Tour Through the Whole Island of Great Britain*, Penguin, Harmondsworth, 1971, 414–16.

18. Betty Brammer, *The Holland Fen: Social and Topographical Changes in a Fenland Environment, 1750–1945*; PhD Thesis, Centre for English Local History, University of Leicester, 2009, 47–8.

19. Joan Thirsk, 'Fenland Farming in the Sixteenth Century', Department of English Local History Occasional Papers No. 3, University College of Leicester, 1953, 44–5.

20. Arthur Young, *General View of the Agriculture of Lincolnshire*, David and Charles, Newton Abbot, Devon, 1970 (first published 1813), 22–3.

21. Betty Brammer, *The Holland Fen*, 22.

Chapter 10

1. Leigh Shaw-Taylor, a historian who believes that the importance of the common has been exaggerated nationally, concedes that the best evidence as to the continued importance of the common in early modern England comes from the Fens, and that 'the preponderance of fen and marsh commons in villages with evidence of high proportions of labourers keeping cows is striking'. Leigh Shaw-Taylor, 'Labourers, Cows, Common Rights and Enclosure', *Past and Present*, 171, 2001, 99–100, 116.

2. Leigh Shaw-Taylor, 'Labourers, Cows, Common Rights and Enclosure', 114; Jane Humphries, 'Enclosures, Common Rights, and Women: The Proletarianization of Families in the Late Eighteenth and Early Nineteenth Centuries', *The Journal of Economic History*, Vol. L, No. 1, March 1990, 24; J.M. Neeson, *Commoners: Common Right, Enclosure and Social Change in England, 1700–1820*, Cambridge University Press, 1996, 311.

3. Arthur Young, *General View of the Agriculture of Lincolnshire*, 468–9.

4. Peter Linebaugh, *The Magna Carta Manifesto: Liberties and Commons for All*, University of California Press, 2008, 65; David Bollier, *Think Like a Commoner: A Short Introduction to the Life of the Commons*, New Society Publishers, Gabriola Island,

Canada, 2014, 91; Jane Humphries, 'Enclosures, Common Rights, and Women: The Proletarianization of Families in the Late Eighteenth and Early Nineteenth Centuries', *The Journal of Economic History*, Vol. L, No. 1, March 1990, 17; E.P. Thompson, 'The Moral Economy of the English Crowd in the Eighteenth Century', *Past and Present*, No. 50, February 1971, 115–16; John Bohstedt, 'Gender, Household and Community Politics: Women in English Riots 1790–1810', *Past and Present*, No. 120, August 1988, 88–122; Elizabeth Foyster, 'Gender Relations', in Barry Coward, ed., *A Companion to Stuart Britain*, Blackwell Publishers, 2003, 121–3.

5. Jane Humphries, 'Enclosures, Common Rights, and Women: The Proletarianization of Families in the Late Eighteenth and Early Nineteenth Centuries', *The Journal of Economic History*, Vol. L, No. 1, March 1990, 47.

6. Neeson has observed that: 'It is no accident that the loudest complaints about the unavailability of commoners for work come from the Hampshire downs and the East Anglian fens' – the areas where common resources were the richest. J.M. Neeson, *Commoners: Common Right, Enclosure and Social Change in England, 1700–1820*, Cambridge University Press, 1996, 177–8.

7. Arthur Young, *General View of the Agriculture of Lincolnshire*, 451.

8. James C. Scott, *Against the Grain: A Deep History of the Earliest States*, Yale University Press, New Haven and London, 2017, 20.

9. Valerie Gerrard, *The Story of the Fens*, Robert Hale, London, 2003, 73.

10. Ian D. Rotherham, *The Lost Fens: England's Greatest Ecological Disaster*, The History Press, Stroud, 2013, 81–6.

11. Daniel Defoe, *A Tour Through the Whole Island of Great Britain*, Penguin, Harmondsworth, 1971, 101.

12. Ian D. Rotherham, *The Lost Fens*, 69.

13. Oliver Rackham, *The History of the Countryside*, Weidenfeld & Nicolson, London, 1993 (first published 1986), 394.

14. Peter Linebaugh, *The Magna Carta Manifesto: Liberties and Commons for All*, University of California Press, 2008, 219.

15. L. Jenyns, *Observations in Meteorology*, 1858; S.B.J. Skertchly, *Geology of the Fenland*, 1877, cited in H.C. Darby, *The Draining of the Fens*, Cambridge University Press, 1940, 241–2; Mary Chamberlain, *Fenwomen: A Portrait of Women in an English Village*, Routledge and Kegan Paul, London 1985 (first published 1975), 30.

16. Arthur Young, *General View of the Agriculture of Lincolnshire*, 22–3, 39, 149–50; Arthur Young, *Annals of Agriculture*, cited in H.C. Darby, *The Draining of the Fens*, Cambridge University Press, 1940, 175.

17. J.M. Heathcote, *Reminiscences of Fen and Mere*, Spottiswode and Co., London, 1876, cited in Ian D. Rotherham, *The Lost Fens: England's Greatest Ecological Disaster*, The History Press, Stroud 2013, 34.

18. Daniel Defoe, *A Tour Through the Whole Island of Great Britain*, Penguin, Harmondsworth, 1971, 417.

19. Jeremy Purseglove, *Taming the Flood: A History and Natural History of Rivers and Wetlands*, Oxford University Press, 1988, 10–11, 100, 301.

20. *Ibid.*, 301.

21. W.B. Stonehouse, *The History and Topography of the Isle of Axholme*, London, Longman, Rees, Orme and Co., 1839, 34.

22. Henry Peet, *Horbling Registers*, Thomas Brakell, Liverpool, 1895, 178.

23. W.H. Wheeler, *The History of the Fens of South Lincolnshire*, second edition, 1888 (first published 1868), 46–7.

24. Steve Hindle, 'Power, Poor Relief, and Social Relations in Holland Fen, c. 1600–1800', *The Historical Journal*, 41, 1998, 67–96.

25. Frances Fox Piven and Richard A. Cloward, *Regulating the Poor: The Functions of Public Welfare*, Vintage Books, 1972, 22.

Chapter 11

1. Peter Linebaugh, *The Magna Carta Manifesto: Liberties and Commons for All*, University of California Press, 2008, 50–1.

2. W.G. Hoskins and L. Dudley Stamp, *The Common Lands of England and Wales*, Collins, London, 1963, 10–11. The authors were members of the Royal Commission on Common Land (1955–58).

3. Peter Linebaugh, *The Magna Carta Manifesto*, 278–9.

4. John Clare, *Emmonsales Heath*.

5. Nicola Whyte, *Inhabiting the Landscape: Place, Custom and Memory, 1500–1800*, Windgather Press, Oxford, 2009, 7, 20.

6. J.M. Neeson, *Commoners: Common Right, Enclosure and Social Change in England, 1700–1820*, Cambridge University Press, 1996, 182.

7. *Ibid.*, 180–1.

8. Nicola Whyte, *Inhabiting the Landscape*, 133–4.

9. Arthur Young, *Annals of Agriculture*, 1805, 543, cited in H.C. Darby, *The Draining of the Fens*, Cambridge University Press, 1940, 174–6.

10. Wesley wrote to The Society for Promoting Christian Knowledge in 1701 that no more than twenty people attended his monthly service of holy communion out of a population of 7,000. He might have exaggerated both the low attendance and those with access to the church to increase his chance of being given extra resources, but even allowing for this, it is clear that not many people went to church! Ralph Waller, *John Wesley: A Personal Portrait*, SPCK, London 2003, 7.

11. Nicola Whyte, *Inhabiting the Landscape*, 45–52.

12. Arthur Young, *General View of the Agriculture of Lincolnshire*, 488–90.

13. Peter Linebaugh, *The Magna Carta Manifesto*, 71–2.

14. Maureen James, *Cambridgeshire Folk Tales*, The History Press, Stroud, 2014, 62–3.

15. Colin Ella, *Myths and Legends of the Isle of Axholme*, Chronicle Publications, 2003, 68.

16. Sir William Dugdale's Diary, 1657, reproduced in H.C. Darby, *The Draining of the Fens*, Cambridge University Press, 1940, Appendix III, 275.

17. Maureen James, *Cambridgeshire Folk Tales*, 28–31.

18. Walter White, *Eastern England from the Thames to the Humber*, Chapman and Hall, 1865, 260.

19. Ian D. Rotherham, *The Lost Fens*, 29.

20. Mary Chamberlain, *Fenwomen: A Portrait of Women in an English Village*, Routledge and Kegan Paul, London, 1985 (first published 1975), 30. Interview with Mary Coe aged 86.

21. Letter to Thomas Rankin from John Wesley, 9 October 1766, *The Works of John Wesley*, Vol. XIII, fourth edition, London, John Mason, 1841, 155.

22. Heather Falvey, *Custom, Resistance and Politics: Local Experiences of Improvement in Early Modern England*, PhD Thesis, University of Warwick, Department of History, 2007, 359–60. For a detailed history of 'camping', the East Anglian form of football which was played in the Fens, see David Dymond, 'A Lost Social Institution: The Camping Close', *Rural History*, 1, 1990, 165–92.

23. Christopher Marlowe, *Legends of the Fenland People*, E.P. Publishing, Wakefield, 1976 (first published Cecil Palmer, 1926), xi–xii.

24. Ian D. Rotherham, *The Lost Fens*, 37.

25. James C. Scott, *Against the Grain: A Deep History of the Earliest States*, Yale University Press, New Haven and London, 2017, 92.

Chapter 12

1. Ian F.W. Beckett, 'The Amateur Military Tradition in Britain', *War and Society*, Vol. 4, 1986.

2. E.P. Thompson, *Whigs and Hunters: The Origin of the Black Act*, Allen Lane, London, 1975, 21–3.

3. J.M. Neeson, *Commoners: Common Right, Enclosure and Social Change in England, 1700–1820*, Cambridge University Press, 1996, 329.

4. Anon. (John Maynard?), *The Anti-Projector: Or The History of the Fen Project*, 1653?.

5. W.H. Wheeler, *The History of the Fens of South Lincolnshire*, second edition, 1888 (first published 1868), 283.

6. Sarah Speight, 'Localising History 1940–1965: The Extra-Mural Contribution', *Journal of Educational Administration and History*, 35, 1, 2003, 51–64; W.H. Hosford, 'Some Lincolnshire Enclosure Documents', *The Economic History Review*, 2, 1, 1949, 73–9.

7. W.H. Hosford, 'Some Lincolnshire Enclosure Documents', 73–9.

8. Hosford's impression was that Horbling property had been bought by 'mostly professional men, merchants and small tradesmen of various types, and also prosperous farmers – all of whom found the purchase of land a convenient way of investing reserves and savings. They probably had an eye on the profits that would ultimately arise from an enclosure, and in some instances they seem to have been the real promoters of the enclosure.' W.H. Hosford, 'Some Lincolnshire Enclosure Documents', 73–9.

9. W.H. Hosford, 'Some Lincolnshire Enclosure Documents', 73–9.

10. Betty Brammer, *The Holland Fen: Social and Topographical Changes in a Fenland Environment, 1750–1945*, PhD Thesis, Centre for English Local History, University of Leicester, 2009, 51.

11. *Ibid.*, 52–3.

12. *Ibid.*, 53–5.

13. *Ibid.*, 63–4.

14. *Ibid.*, 63–5.

15. *Ibid.*, 67.

16. *Ibid.*, 68–9.

17. *Ibid.*, 69.

18. *Ibid.*, 69–70.

19. *Ibid.*, 70.

20. *London Gazette*, 1–5 August 1769, cited in Steve Hindle, 'Power, Poor Relief, and Social Relations in Holland Fen, c. 1600–1800', *The Historical Journal*, 41, 1998, 67–96.

21. Betty Brammer, *The Holland Fen*, 70.

22. Steve Hindle, 'Power, Poor Relief, and Social Relations in Holland Fen, c. 1600–1800', *The Historical Journal*, 41, 1998, 67–96.

23. Betty Brammer, *The Holland Fen*, 70.

24. Robert Carter, *Some Strictures on the Ancholme Drainage Addressed to the Smaller Non-Commissioned Freeholders and Occupiers of Land in that Level*, M. Wood, Lincoln, 1772, 3–6.

25. *Ibid.*, 30–1.

26. Ian D. Rotherham, *The Lost Fens: England's Greatest Ecological Disaster*, The History Press, Stroud, 2013, 75.

27. H.C. Darby, *The Draining of the Fens*, Cambridge University Press, 1940, 152.

28. Ian D. Rotherham, *The Lost Fens*, 144.

29. William White, *History, Gazetter and Directory of Norfolk*, 1836, 687; Leigh Shaw-Taylor, 'Labourers, Cows, Common Rights and Enclosure', *Past and Present*, 171, 2001, 118.

30. Karl Marx, *Capital: A Critical Analysis of Capitalist Production*, translated from the third German edition by Samuel Moore and Edward Aveling and edited by Frederick Engels, first English edition, London, 1886, 643–5.

31. Peter Linebaugh argues that: 'Together the expelled commoners and the captured Africans provided the labor power available for exploitation in the factories of the field (tobacco and sugar) and the factories for the towns (woollens and cottons).' Peter Linebaugh, *The Magna Carta Manifesto: Liberties and Commons for All*, University of California Press, 2008, 94–5.

32. Steve Hindle, 'Power, Poor Relief, and Social Relations in Holland Fen', 67–96.

33. William Cobbett, *Rural Rides*, Volume 2, Dent, 1912; Edward Storey, *Letters from the Fens*, Robert Hale, Oxford, 1998, 254–6.

34. *Ibid.*

35. Alun Howkins, 'Poor Labouring Men: Rural Radicalism in Norfolk 1872–1923', Routledge and Kegan Paul, London, 1985, 143, 166–8. Alice Rushmer recalled that 'They were paying our men here more to go up there [to Norfolk] than they were paying their own men, just to make their own men suffer.' Mary Chamberlain, *Fenwomen: A Portrait of Women in an English Village*, Routledge and Kegan Paul, London, 1985 (first published 1975), 80.

36. Mary Chamberlain, *Fenwomen: A Portrait of Women in an English Village*, Routledge and Kegan Paul, London, 1985 (first published 1975), 29.

37. An older woman in Isleham recalls that widows used to ask for their dole until the Second World War – when presumably social welfare reforms made the custom redundant. Mary

Chamberlain, *Fenwomen: A Portrait of Women in an English Village*, Routledge and Kegan Paul, London, 1985 (first published 1975), 149.

Chapter 13

1. Camden's *Britannia* was first published in 1586. The quotes are taken from the 1637 edition.

2. W. Pennington, *Reflections on the Various Advantages Resulting from the Draining, Inclosing and Allotting of Large Commons and Common Fields*, 1769, 37.

3. George Crabbe, *The Village* (1783), in George Crabbe, *Tales: 1812 and Other Selected Poems*, Howard Mills, ed., Cambridge, 1967, 3.

4. Jeremy Purseglove, *Taming the Flood: A History and Natural History of Rivers and Wetlands*, Oxford University Press, 1988, 34.

5. Keith Lindley, *Fenland Riots and the English Revolution*, 58.

6. See Jean Tsushima, 'Melting into the Landscape: The Story of the 17th-century Walloons in the Fens', in Randolph Vigne and Charles Littleton, eds, *From Strangers to Citizens: The Integration of Immigrant Communities in Britain, Ireland and Colonial America, 1550–1750*, Sussex Academic Press, Brighton, 2001.

7. *The Case and Proceedings of at Least Sixty Gentlemen, Participants and Purchasers, for valuable consideration of Lands, in the Level of Hatfield Chase … and More Than Two Hundred of their Tenants who have been despoiled of their Estates, by the inhumane and barbarous Ryots of the Inhabitants of the Mannor of Epworth …*, London, 1654.

8. Heather Falvey, *Custom, Resistance and Politics: Local Experiences of Improvement in Early Modern England*, PhD Thesis, University of Warwick, Department of History, 2007, 59–260.

9. Attributed to Samuel Fortrey, *History of the Narrative of the Great Level of the Fenns Called Bedford Level*, 1685.

10. Joan Thirsk, *English Peasant Farming: The Agrarian History of Lincolnshire from Tudor to Recent Times*, Routledge and Kegan Paul, London, 1957, 37.

11. Anon. (John Maynard?), *The Anti-Projector: Or The History of the Fen Project*, 1653?.

12. Celia Fiennes, *Through England on a Side Saddle in the time of William and Mary being the Diary of Celia Fiennes*, E.W. Griffiths, ed., 1888, 127–31; H.C. Darby, *The Draining of the Fens*, Cambridge University Press, 1940, 111–12.

13. Daniel Defoe, *A Tour Through the Whole Island of Great Britain*, Penguin, Harmondsworth, 1971, 100.

14. In the case of Charles II, not even the most rare and sought-after medicine – the powdered skull of a man that had died but had never been buried – helped, although the Peruvian bark, a source of quinine, could have if it had been given earlier. Ian D. Rotherham, *The Lost Fens: England's Greatest Ecological Disaster*, The History Press, Stroud, 2013, 45.

15. Ian D. Rotherham, *The Lost Fens: England's Greatest Ecological Disaster*, 25; Arthur Young, *Annals of Agriculture*, xliii, 1805, 543; H.C. Darby, *The Draining of the Fens*, 174–6.

16. R. Parkinson, *Agriculture of the County of Huntingdon*, 1811, 21; W. Watson, *An Historical Account … of Wisbech*, 1827; H.C. Darby, *The Draining of the Fens*, 180. Malaria became progressively less common during the nineteenth century, with

the last domestic case contracted in Kent in 1918. The reasons for this decline are not as clear as is easily assumed, given that during this period the relevant mosquito remained widespread. Oliver Rackham, *The History of the Countryside*, Weidenfeld & Nicolson, London, 1993 (first published 1986), 389.

17. J.M. Neeson, *Commoners: Common Right, Enclosure and Social Change in England, 1700–1820*, Cambridge University Press, 1996, 43–7.

18. J.L. Hammond and Barbara Hammond, *The Village Labourer*, 1911, reprinted 1966, 30–4.

19. Susanna Wade Martins, *Farmers, Landlords and Landscapes: Rural Britain, 1720 to 1820*, Windgather Press, Bollington, Cheshire, 2004, 9.

20. Arthur Young, *Agriculture of the County of Lincoln*, 1813; Jeremy Purseglove, *Taming the Flood*, 34.

21. *The Gazetteer and Directory of the County of Huntingdon*, 1854, 76.

22. Ian D. Rotherham, *The Lost Fens*, 35.

23. Joel Mokyr, *The Enlightened Economy: An Economic History of Britain 1700–1850*, Yale University Press, New Haven and London, 2009, 174–5.

24. Joan Thirsk, *Fenland Farming in the Sixteenth Century*, Department of English Local History Occasional Papers No. 3, University College of Leicester, 1953, 9.

25. J.M. Neeson, *Commoners: Common Right, Enclosure and Social Change in England*, 41.

26. Derek Wall, *The Commons in History: Culture, Conflict and Ecology*, The MIT Press, Cambridge, Massachusetts, 2014,

65; Adam Smith, *The Wealth of Nations*, 1937 edition (first published 1776); J.M. Neeson, *Commoners: Common Right, Enclosure and Social Change in England*, 67–8.

27. J.M. Neeson, *Commoners: Common Right, Enclosure and Social Change in England*, 48–9.

28. W.H. Wheeler, *The History of the Fens of South Lincolnshire*, 46–7.

Chapter 14

1. William Cobbett, *Rural Rides*, Volume 2, Dent 1912; cited in Edward Storey, *Letters from the Fens*, Robert Hale, 1998, Oxford, 93.

2. For more information see www.yaxleyhistory.org

3. H.C. Darby, *The Draining of the Fens*, Cambridge University Press, 1940, 220–30.

4. Susanna Wade Martins, *Farmers, Landlords and Landscapes: Rural Britain, 1720 to 1820*, Windgather Press, Bollington, Cheshire, 2004, 61–2, 144.

5. Charles Kingsley, in *Prose Idylls*, quoted in the *Leisure Hour*, 26 May 1877, cited in Ian D. Rotherham, *The Lost Fens: England's Greatest Ecological Disaster*, The History Press, Stroud, 2013, 32.

Chapter 15

1. Christopher Taylor, *The Cambridgeshire Landscape: Cambridgeshire and the Southern Fens*, Hodder and Stoughton, London, 1973, 199.

2. W. Gooch, *Agriculture of the County of Cambridge*, 1813, 246.

3. Celia Fiennes, *Through England on a Side Saddle in the time of William and Mary being the Diary of Celia Fiennes*, E.W. Griffiths, ed., 1888, 127–31; H.C. Darby, *The Draining of the Fens*, Cambridge University Press, 1940, 111–12.

4. In 1724, Defoe observed that in the Fens 'are some wonderful engines for throwing up water, and such as are not to be seen anywhere else, whereof one in particular threw up (as they assur'd us) twelve hundred ton of water in half an hour, and goes by windsails, 12 wings or sails to a mill …'. Daniel Defoe, *A Tour Through the Whole Island of Great Britain*, Penguin, Harmondsworth, 1971, 417.

5. Jeremy Purseglove, *Taming the Flood: A History and Natural History of Rivers and Wetlands*, Oxford University Press, 1988, 58–9.

6. Arthur Young, *Annals of Agriculture*, xliii, 1805, 539–43.

7. Jim Hargan, 'The Fens below Sea Level', *English Heritage*, 2007.

8. Arthur Young, *Annals of Agriculture*, xliii, 1805, 543; H.C. Darby, *The Draining of the Fens*, 172–3, 179.

9. Susanna Wade Martins, *Farmers, Landlords and Landscapes: Rural Britain, 1720 to 1820*, Windgather Press, Bollington, Cheshire, 2004, 14; Alan Harris, 'Changes in the Early Railway Age: 1800–1850', in H.C. Darby, ed., *A New Historical Geography of England*, Cambridge University Press, 1973, 482–4.

10. Susanna Wade Martins, *Farmers, Landlords and Landscapes*, 14, 63.

11. Susanna Wade Martins, *Farmers, Landlords and Landscapes*, 62; Joan Thirsk, *English Peasant Farming: The Agrarian History of Lincolnshire from Tudor to Recent Times*, Routledge and Kegan Paul, London, 1957, 314–5.

12. Joan Thirsk, *English Peasant Farming*, 7, 42.

13. *Ibid.*, 317.

14. H. Rider Haggard, *Rural England*, 186.

15. Thomas Edward Scrutton, *Commons and Common Fields or The History and Policy of the Laws Relating to Commons and Enclosures in England*, Cambridge University Press, 1887, 9, 154.

16. W.G. Hoskins and L. Dudley Stamp, *The Common Lands of England and Wales*, Collins, London, 1963, 65. Both the National Trust for Places of Historic Interest and Natural Beauty (1894) and the Society for the Promotion of Nature Reserves (1912) grew out of the commons preservation movement. See J. Sheil, *Nature in Trust: The History of Nature Conservation in Britain*, Glasgow, 1976.

17. Jeremy Purseglove, *Taming the Flood*, 93.

18. Susanna Wade Martins, *Farmers, Landlords and Landscapes*, 63; J.M. Neeson, *Commoners: Common Right, Enclosure and Social Change in England, 1700–1820*, Cambridge University Press, 1996, 47–8.

19. Joan Thirsk, *English Peasant Farming*, 317–18.

20. Karl Marx, *Capital: A Critical Analysis of Capitalist Production*, translated from the third German edition by Samuel Moore and Edward Aveling and edited by Frederick Engels, London, 1886, 675.

21. J.M. Neeson, *Commoners: Common Right, Enclosure and Social Change in England*, 292.

22. E.P. Thompson, *The Making of the English Working Class*, Penguin, Harmondsworth, 1968, 253.

23. J.M. Neeson, *Commoners: Common Right, Enclosure and Social Change in England*, 291–2.

24. See James Boyce, *Van Diemen's Land*, Black Inc, Melbourne, 2008.

25. E.A.R. Ennion, *Adventurers Fen*, Methuen and Co., London, 1942, 12.

26. *Ibid.*, 1–2, 9–13.

27. Mary Coe, aged 86, recalled in the early 1970s that when she was young, 'No one left the village [of Isleham]. And there were no outsiders in the village either … If there was a stranger about, you wanted to know who they were, and were they come from.' Even at the time the interviews were done, with cars far from universal and public transport services reduced, the level of isolation revealed by Mary Chamberlain is extraordinary. Many women rarely left the village and some young mothers of schoolchildren had never been to London or another big city. Mary Chamberlain, *Fenwomen: A Portrait of Women in an English Village*, Routledge and Kegan Paul, London, 1985 (first published 1975), 149.

28. Alan Everitt, 'Non Conformity in Country Parishes', in Joan Thirsk, ed., *Land, Church and People: Essays Presented to Professor H.P.R. Finberg*, British Agricultural History Society, 1970, 183, 197.

29. E.A.R. Ennion, *Adventurers Fen*, 9.

30. Alan Everitt, 'Non Conformity in Country Parishes', 197–8.

31. Linda Colley, *Britons: Forging the Nation 1707–1837*, Yale University Press, New Haven, 1992, 291–3.

32. Mary Chamberlain, *Fenwomen: A Portrait of Women in an English Village*, Routledge and Kegan Paul, London, 1985 (first published 1975), 146.

33. Charles Kingsley, *Prose Idylls*, 1873.

Chapter 16

1. E.A.R. Ennion, *Adventurers Fen*, Methuen and Co., London, 1942, vii.

2. *Ibid.*, 13.

3. Jeremy Purseglove, *Taming the Flood: A History and Natural History of Rivers and Wetlands*, Oxford University Press, 1988, 5, 68–71.

4. Peter Hewitt, *Fenland: A Landscape made by Man*, Wisbech Society and Preservation Trust, 2014, 24.

5. Ian D. Rotherham, *The Lost Fens: England's Greatest Ecological Disaster*, The History Press, Stroud, 2013, 145.

6. Jim Hargan, 'The Fens below Sea Level', *English Heritage*, 2007.

7. Ian D. Rotherham, *The Lost Fens*, 193.

8. Paul Middleton, *England's Lost Lake: The Story of Whittlesea Mere*, Fast Print Publishing, Peterborough, 2018, 10–12.

9. The level of poverty in Isleham in the post-war decades is conveyed in Mary Chamberlain, *Fenwomen: A Portrait of Women in an English Village*, Routledge and Kegan Paul, London, 1985 (first published 1975), especially 41–3, 78–80.

10. W.G. Hoskins and L. Dudley Stamp, *The Common Lands of England and Wales*, Collins, London, 1963, 119, 255.

11. *Ibid.*, 119–20.

12. *Ibid.*, 115.

13. *Ibid.*

14. *Ibid.*

15. Garrett Hardin, 'The Tragedy of the Commons', *Science*, Vol. 162, December 1968, 1243–48. See also David Bollier, *Think Like a Commoner: A Short Introduction to the Life of the Commons*, New Society Publishers, Gabriola Island, Canada, 2014, 2.

16. In 1990 Elinor Ostrom published *Governing the Commons*, which set out basic design principles of successful commons. Ostrom was awarded the Nobel Prize for Economics in 2009, the year after the global financial crisis, 'for her analysis of economic governance, especially the commons'.

Postscript

1. H.C. Darby, *The Draining of the Fens*, Cambridge University Press, 1940, 34–5.

2. Anon, *An Enquiry into the Advantages and Disadvantages resulting from Bills of Inclosure ...*, 1780, 66–7, cited in H.C. Darby, *The Draining of the Fens*, 38–9.

3. R.H. Tawney, 'Introduction' in Joan Thirsk, *Fenland Farming in the Sixteenth Century*, Department of English Local History Occasional Papers No. 3, University College of Leicester, 1953, 1–6.

4. Peter Linebaugh and Marcus Rediker, *The Many-Headed Hydra: Sailors, Slaves, Commoners, and the Hidden History of the Revolutionary Atlantic*, Beacon Press, Boston, 2000, 20–1.

5. Karl Polanyi, *The Great Transformation: The Political and Economic Origins of Our Time*, Beacon Press, Boston, 2001 (first published 1944), 39–40.

6. W.H. Wheeler, *The History of the Fens of South Lincolnshire*, 36–8.

INDEX